ENDORSEMENTS

Anyone who has studied the global environmental movement has no doubt heard the term "Gaia." Gaia is a revival of paganism that rejects Christianity, considers Christianity its biggest enemy, and views the Christian faith as its only obstacle to a global religion centered on Gaia worship and the uniting of all life forms around the goddess of "Mother Earth." A cunning mixture of science, paganism, Eastern mysticism, and feminism has made this pagan cult a growing threat to the Christian Church. Gaia worship is at the very heart of today's green movement. This religious movement, with cult-like qualities, is being promoted by leading figures and organizations proclaiming the deity of Earth and blames the falling away from this pagan god on the environmentally unfriendly followers of Jesus Christ.

The United Nations and more recently, Petrus Romanus, have been extremely successful in infusing the "Green Theology" into an international governmental body that has an increasing affect and control over all of our lives and, Sheila's book could not be more timely.

—**Dr. Tom Horn,** author of *Petrus Romanus*

The Green Movement and the worship of Gaia is the ultimate expression of goddess worship. The woman who rides the beast in the book of Revelation is once again empowering her occult adherents to destroy the earth under the guise of saving it! The Bible states that the God of heaven will destroy those who destroy the earth! "The Green Man," a chimera like visage, whether associated with Bacchus or ancient fertility symbols is steeped in paganism and the green movement is the ultimate expression of worshipping the creation rather than the Creator!

Sheila unmasks the true supernatural manifesting arm of evil as she reveals the Green Movement and its deeply dangerous harvest that will result in the destruction of several billion lives as it fully manifests itself before our eyes.

—**Stephen Quayle,** author of *Xenogenesis*

The modern greens, a "Down With (Other) People!" movement, is a curious hybrid of doomsday cult and encounter group. Its tenets include that (other) people are pollution, bringing about catastrophe prophesied by computer models that, by the way, will project any future you design them to project; that (other) people should not be born or—if they are—should not be permitted the comforts and safety of hydrocarbon-fueled prosperity.

To attain the greens' eschaton, and while grappling with the reality that no free society would do to itself what these people demand, they shriek that those who dare dissent must be silenced, jailed if necessary.

Despite desperate efforts to rebrand, they are a wealthy, white, Western movement obsessed with using government to impose schemes that harm, and indeed kill by the tens of thousands, the most vulnerable to whom they pay lip service while cruelly grinding them with policies even their own Cassandra-like computer models affirm are climatically meaningless gestures. This ignoble movement is not your father's conservationism.

—**Christopher C. Horner**
New York Times best-selling author of *Red Hot Lies*

GREEN GOSPEL

THE NEW WORLD RELIGION

GREEN GOSPEL

THE NEW WORLD RELIGION

SHEILA ZILINSKY

REDEMPTION
PRESS

Published by Redemption Press, PO Box 427, Enumclaw, WA 98022 Toll Free (844) 2REDEEM (273-3336)

Redemption Press is honored to present this title in partnership with the author. The views expressed or implied in this work are those of the author. Redemption Press provides our imprint seal representing design excellence, creative content and high quality production.

Unless otherwise noted, all Scriptures are taken from the *Holy Bible, New International Version*, Copyright © 1973, 1978, 1984 by the International Bible Society. Used by permission of Zondervan Publishing House. The "niv" and "New International Version" trademarks are registered in the United States Patent and Trademark Office by International Bible Society.

Scripture references marked KJV are taken from the *King James Version* of the Bible.

Scripture references marked NASB are taken from the *New American Standard Bible*, © 1960, 1963, 1968, 1971, 1972, 1973, 1975, 1977 by The Lockman Foundation. Used by permission.

ISBN 13: 978-1-63232-522-8 (Print)
          978-1-63232-524-2 (ePub)
          978-1-63232-525-9 (Mobi)

Library of Congress Catalog Card Number: 2015945677

CONTENTS

FOREWORD

The year 1859 was pivotal in reducing people's ability to understand the world. In that year, Darwin's *The Origin of Species* was published, and Alexander von Humboldt died.

Darwin's theory was used by science to defeat religion, but in doing so it prevented any challenges to the theory's validity. No scientist would dare say Darwin was wrong for fear of giving support to the "creationists." Western society has a view of the world based on an untested scientific theory, a situation that contradicts the basic tenets of scientific scholarship.

Von Humboldt is credited with being the last "universal" person. That is, he was the last person who "knew" all the science and geography known at that time. We still have renaissance people who have a wider knowledge of many subjects, but not universal knowledge.

The result since then is that the proliferation of knowledge, information, and ideas encouraged and lauded specialization and derided generalization. People specialize and become experts in one small piece of a very large, complex puzzle but are incapable of seeing the larger picture necessary for context and real understanding. We are truly in a world where we cannot see the forest for the trees. We have more information and less understanding.

This book addresses this problem by drawing together the various threads to help us understand how and why the real answer, Christianity, is under attack. It explains how various people, groups, and ideologies exploit vulnerabilities of people in a rudderless world. Confusion, fear, and panic are the fertile fields for exploitation and distraction from those who practice evil.

G. K. Chesterton (1874–1936) is identified, among other things, as a lay theologian and Christian apologist. He gave much thought to the human contradictions and the human condition, so some called him "the prince of paradox." His life spanned the beginnings of the impact of Darwin's evolutionary theory and the social implications of Marxism. One of his more important observations was that, "When men choose not to believe in God, they do not thereafter believe in nothing; they then become capable of believing in anything."

In other words, they lose their moral compass and become vulnerable to the siren song of many voices, but especially those that promote atheism.

Osama Bin Laden, mastermind of the 9/11 attack and devout believer in Wahhabism, said that Western society, by which he meant Christianity, had lost its moral direction. Wahhabism is a branch of Sunni Islam created by Muhammad ibn Abd al-Wahhab (1703–1792). He believed Sunni Islam became weak over time, and so he formed this ultraconservative, strictly orthodox branch that promotes a revival of the Koran and early Islam. Most of the Saudi royal family is Wahhabi.

Bin Laden's claim that the West is morally adrift is valid. Of course, he wanted to impose his morality, which is worse than being adrift. However, people need a belief system and a morality.

The moral vacuum created by the rise of atheism because of Darwin's scientific theory and Marxist political and economic theory left young people vulnerable to "believing in anything." This book ties together the various strands, which specialists never pull together. It weaves the torn fabric of our current world and explains why many, especially the rudderless young, are vulnerable to the pantheistic belief system of environmentalism. Most don't know that Christianity already has the answers.

—Dr. Tim Ball

PREFACE

Imagine that everything you have been told about the environment was wrong. What if global warming was a good thing? Imagine that carbon dioxide was essential for life and humans, and plants would die without it. Imagine that "overpopulation" was an illusory problem created to simply cull the population. In biology, culling refers to the process of segregating organisms from a group according to undesired characteristics. Imagine that the climate has always changed by design. What if polar bears, glaciers, rain forests, sea levels, and polar ice caps were all doing just fine? Imagine that economic growth made the world a cleaner, healthier, happier place.

Just imagine that when God created the earth and its contents, He knew exactly what He was doing and didn't need us to run around "saving the planet." Imagine that the world's elite had pushed a convincing lie so big that most humans and governments swallowed it hook, line, and sinker. Imagine that the "green agenda" was an elaborate scheme to eradicate

Christianity and force you to accept a pagan form of pantheism called Gaia worship and complete subjugation to it.

Unfortunately, you don't have to imagine all these things because, astonishingly, this is what is really happening. This book will show you that the green agenda is the grandest of all tyrannical schemes. It will follow the history of the process and its exploitation for the socialist anti-religion agenda.

This book is deliberately not academic. Rather, it grew from a very personal voyage of a Christian woman struggling to understand how and why events have evolved. It is as historically accurate as possible, but it is not written for academics. It is written for the vast majority of people affected by the machinations of the green agenda in as simple and understandable a manner as possible. It represents a personal journey that the author knows from experience and interactions with thousands of people through the Internet, conferences, and informal meetings. It provides context and understanding for a majority of people, but especially Christians. The guidance in this approach is the Bible, which is written so everybody can understand. There is no value to information if people don't understand.

Academics will attack the book and dismiss it as a polemic, that it is an attack on the immoral, intellectual modern society. They are right.

Acknowledgments

I thank the living God Jehovah and the Lord Jesus Christ, whose spirit of truth made this possible.

To my tenacious uncle Wally Patterson, whose boldness to show me many of the discoveries referenced in this book put me on a different course in life. You're one of the few who really get it.

To Dr. Tim Ball, the most wonderful mentor I could ever have the privilege of having. Your bravery and bold stance on the truth inspire me every day. Your contributions to this book are invaluable to me, as is your friendship.

Thank you to Dr. Calvin Beisner for his contribution to this book and his work at http://www.cornwallalliance.org.

To my heroes—Augusto Perez, David Lankford, Steve Quayle, and Tom Horn—four brilliant, bold men of God, who speak the truth amongst a widespread sea of compromise, you inspire me.

To my very good friend Rob Webster, thanks for your wisdom, friendship, encouragement, and love of the Lord.

To the others—my true brothers and sisters in the Lord (especially the watchmen). To you I say keep up the good fight of faith. I know the higher calling of the Lord Jesus Christ is often a very difficult path, but it's definitely worth it.

Finally, to my three beautiful sons, Dallas, Katlin, and Carter, who have endured a lifetime of criticism and incessant conspiracy theorist labeling of the woman who gave them birth. I hope my strength, courage, and love inspire you to always stand up for the truth and to be the men I pray for you to be.

I dedicate this book to you and to those who seek the truth.

INTRODUCTION

There exists a group of clandestine, self-proclaimed ruling oligarchs, who are in fact soulless pagans with designs on reshaping the world into a state of complete global governance where everyone embraces the goddess Gaia as God. Christians are at war with this group and don't even know it. They don't know because the group designed it that way. It is a good example of the Bible's observation in Isaiah 29:15 that the devil's work is done in the darkness.

The West is being radically transformed into a soulless, ungodly Marxist society. America is not the last bastion of freedom; it is the first and the only one. For that, it is under attack as it represents everything the Founding Fathers envisioned, a nation of free people under God. Public education and the progressive mainstream media have indoctrinated Americans to accept a cabal's collectivist Marxist ideas as a valid part of the American way. They are not. They are diametrically opposed to the Constitutional Republic and liberties established by our Founding Fathers on fundamental moral tenets of biblical law. Their endgame is to destroy constitutional liberties and the free market economy through deindustrialization and ultimately population reduction. Even more frightening is their astonishing plan to reinstate a form of paganism dating back to Nimrod. These people want to control every aspect of your life and to exert dominance over every single daily activity. Their astonishing goal is to eradicate the one person who stands in their way: Jesus Christ.

This book will explain how the claim that human-induced or anthropogenic global warming (AGW) and the green agenda were deliberately hatched decades ago as the basis for this political agenda and actually have nothing at all to do with science or the environment. The green agenda is not about "saving the planet" as its creators are so quick to spout; it is instead a pagan imperial doctrine to justify wiping out nation states and reducing world population in order to secure the continued world rule by the British Empire and the privately-controlled cabal behind the green agenda.

Those pushing the global warming fraud have targeted human CO_2 emissions as its ostensible cause because CO_2, or carbon dioxide, is the God-given natural and necessary by-product of the industrial activity that sustains human life— energy, agriculture, manufacturing, etc. Pope Francis doesn't realize that in his latest attack on climate change and fossil fuels he is condemning the poor to continued deprivation and misery. Sadly, history shows that all these objectives are designed to control people completely, to keep them enslaved by making simple survival a daily challenge, with no time to think.

Over the past two decades, the progressively built hysteria about global warming has now erupted into a full-blown public relations offensive. Al Gore, the Pope, the British Royal Family and their intimates, among others, are leading the push for a One World Climate Regime, which if fully implemented would be hell on earth in the form of a totalitarian government. Elaine Dewar explained in her book, *Cloak of Green* how the chief architect of the environmental and global warming agenda, Maurice Strong, "was using the UN [United Nations] as a platform to sell a global environment crisis and the Global Governance Agenda."[1]

Even more insidious is the fact that this cabal of collectivists has discovered the ultimate vehicle to force their pagan New World Order Green Religion upon the entire world: the collective fear that the sky is falling, and only they can save the world. As H. L. Mencken explained, "The urge to save humanity is almost always a false front for the urge to rule." The US Founding Fathers understood this urge and used the US Constitution to prevent control of the people by government. As Thomas Paine wrote in *Common Sense* (1776),

> This new world hath been the asylum for the persecuted lovers of civil and religious liberty from every part of Europe. Hither have they fled, not from the tender embraces of the mother, but from the cruelty of the monster; and it is so far true of England, that the same tyranny which drove the first emigrants from home pursues their descendants still.

---

[1] http://sacpa.ca/userfile/file/Lethbridge%20Actual%201.pdf.

xix

CHAPTER 1

WATERMELONS: GREEN ON THE OUTSIDE, RED ON THE INSIDE

The title of this book is deliberately ambiguous. Environmentalists think it is a book that will explain and praise their worldview. It is only after you read the preface that a completely different interpretation appears. This notion that the outside does not reflect the inside, or what is actually happening, is expressed in various analogies. The common one for extreme environmentalism is that people are watermelons, promoting a green environmentalism on the outside, but underneath they are promoting a red socialist agenda. I contend that it is more than a political agenda because socialism is atheistic and anti-Christian. Since people need a belief system, they have converted environmentalism into a new form of pagan religion.

THE DEVELOPMENT OF TOTALITARIANISM

Most people think that totalitarianism is "right-wing" dictatorships, but there is totalitarianism of the left as well.

Indeed, the most ruthless dictatorships are left-wing. Hitler founded the NAZIS, which is an abbreviation of the National Socialist Party.

When asked who they think was the most evil political figure of the twentieth century, most people suggest it was Hitler. Surprisingly, it wasn't; it was Josef Stalin. He killed even more millions of people and was far more evil and ruthless than Hitler. Today a deluge of evidence about the bloody horrors of Stalin's rule is emerging from Russian archives.

In 1917, thanks to Lenin, the official reign of communist terror began with a simple red flag heralding victory; that blood-red flag became the lasting color and symbol of communism. Lenin's Russia would transition to Stalin's Soviet Union. During the ensuing seventy years, over 110 million people were exterminated around the world, but mostly in the Soviet Union, in the name of Marxism. The diabolical tentacles of Marxism have steadily reached into the West for decades. The question is, what does an evil, tyrannical dictator with a callous disregard for human life have to do with global warming?

In order to help you understand the green agenda, we must start the story with Karl Marx, a very sinister and diabolical man. He was born in Trier, Germany, on May 5, 1818, and lived for sixty-five years, during which time his twisted mind conceived atrocious plots to infect the world with his godless philosophies. Karl Marx, a self-admitted Satanist, fashioned himself as a scientist, coming up with crazed, deranged laws of matter that supported what many elitists believe; that those with better brains have a responsibility to the world to rule over those with inferior brains because, left to their own devices, those inferior-brained people would kill each other and destroy the planet.

Science suited the agenda because it is amoral and apolitical. It was given academic legitimacy by Darwin's evolutionary theory. In other words, Marx believed that those born with a better brain had the right to rule others. The paradox of this elitism is lost on socialists and communists who promote the belief that all people are equal with equal opportunities. In recent decades, more and more Americans have been conditioned by politicians to depend on government to solve their problems.

This is how demagogues have always operated. They demonize something or someone, in this case "the rich," implying they obtained their wealth by exploiting the downtrodden; they stir up racial hatreds at every opportunity; they endlessly bash capitalists as evil exploiters; and they promise "social justice" and universal happiness if only we will elevate them to power over us. They do all this by appealing to anger and envy. They know instinctively that if they can stir up and ignite these dark and addictive passions in all of us, they will create a large voting bloc of people dependent on them, and thus be rewarded with great power. In its purest form, this phenomenon is called Marxism, but variously communism or socialism. Regardless, the spiritual core is raw envy. The practical political core is complete suppression and control of the individual.

Academics argue, irrelevantly, that these are different, but the common denominator is they all advocate total control by government. This philosophy of cradle-to-grave security and "wealth redistribution" exerts a powerfully seductive grip on people who have not discovered true inner "government." As William Penn famously said, "Men must be governed by God or they will be ruled by tyrants."

Communism, of course, is atheistic—where the government is the only true god, the giver of blessings, the solver of problems, the dispenser of justice and mercy. This envy-based, class warfare-fueled revolutionary system promulgates justice, fairness, and progress; but sadly, the only progress it delivers is slavery. This is the appeal more and more Americans have been conditioned to over the years. We have progressively fallen away from the Judeo-Christian values that once animated our culture and institutions. The envy-based, pseudo ideology system that Marx unleashed on the world is alive and well and, in different forms, dominates large parts of the world. In America, it has taken deep root in the left wing of the Democratic Party.

Ronald Reagan may have been instrumental in destroying the "evil empire" of the Soviet Union, but you cannot destroy evil itself. Evil remains and continues to do its job of tempting and corrupting the souls of men. It is the most evil of all, the evil within. This includes a litany of moral degradation including the encouragement of immorality—free sex, abortion, homosexuality, easy divorce, and so on. These moral failings are part and parcel of the socialist modus operandi, because immoral, dysfunctional people who have crossed the moral line, thus becoming estranged from God, now need the "god" of socialist government. All of this is what is now occurring in the United States as a few socialist politicians masquerading as Democrats establish control through the bureaucracies. All of this is what we now have inherited in the person of Barack Hussein Obama, who occupies the office of president of the USA.

Obama's selection and appointment was constructed to advance a socialist agenda. Americans on the whole have become increasingly corrupted over the years. They've been conditioned into voting for unprincipled, unscrupulous charlatans who believe the Saul Alinsky dictum that the end justifies the means. If it takes lies, then that is acceptable.

We almost elected Al Gore, the man with a penchant for chicanery and outlandish deceptions, as president—who, as my book explains, refuses to debate. He incessantly repeats the "science is settled" mantra and chants nonsensical claims that we are in a "climate crisis." Gore insists that those refusing to acknowledge his views must be dealt with in the harshest manner, as any dictator would urge. It is a classic example of the socialist belief that if you are not with me, you must be against me. If anyone dares question or even disagree, he or she is an enemy of the cause, which in socialist terms is the State. The real science community, contrary to Gore's politically motivated claims, knows the earth has actually been cooling for the last eighteen years. The question is why would they lie to us? In this book we will explain how and why.

MARXIST IDEOLOGY

It is critical to know that the ideas of Karl Marx and Frederick Engels appealed to the founders of collectivism because it contradicts a structure founded on belief in God. Rather, founders of collectivism promote a moral system of knowledge through advanced education and believe they can become masters of the universe with no room for anything other than their so-called absolute truth. For them, God is a mythical crutch for millions of plebs, and whatever morality is required shall be defined by them subject to their goals. As Marx put it, religion is the opiate of the masses. Telling a lie or perpetrating a fraud is perfectly acceptable as long as the end justifies the means. This parallels the Islamic belief that a lie is acceptable to advance the doctrine. This tolerance of lying marks a fundamental break with Christianity in which lying is morally wrong and breaks the trust between individuals. Christianity underscores the sense of personal responsibility that God provided and is inherent in the US Constitution.

Karl Marx began his rebellion against God as a student at the University of Berlin where he was strongly influenced by the philosopher George Hegel and his followers known as the young Hegelians. Their goal was straightforward—eliminate Christianity. Marx and his followers loathed the republican form of government, especially the American manifestation. They were determined to eradicate the Western Christian simpletons and their philosophy of individualism that was the antithesis of collectivism. The ideals were encapsulated in the phrase, "life, liberty, and the pursuit of happiness" and incorporated in the United States Declaration of Independence. America's founders understood that property was synonymous with liberty and security in a free-market economic system with minimal government regulation. Such beliefs were offensive to Marx.

The concept of a God who would command humans to take ownership of land, improve it, and even defend that property as their own completely contradicted his state-controlled ideology. In 1848, Marx and Engels presented their final formula for world revolution, which they called the Communist Manifesto. In chapter 2 they boldly stated the central objective of a new world order—the abolition of private property. Destroying the foundations of property and a capitalist economy was the ultimate goal and so every option was on the table. Without religion there was no moral limit on lying, cheating, and murder because "the end justifies the means." It is summarized in the old joke about the revolutionary speaking to a large audience about what will happen after the revolution. He lists a series of changes and then, speaking to the white collar/blue collar dichotomy, he says, "Come the revolution, we will all wear shirts and ties."

A voice in the crowd says, "I don't want to wear a shirt and a tie," to which the speaker replies, "Come the revolution, you will do what you are told."

Few people know that the failure of state control of land under communism occurred very shortly after the 1917 Russian Revolution. The seizing of land and the creation of massive state-controlled farms were the first actions. Within a couple of years, food supply was falling and undermining the entire economy. The fact that hungry people will rise up against bad government is the trigger for most revolutions. People tolerate bad government because they know there is no good government. The two major reasons that will make them act are failure of the food supply and when the leaders forget they only govern at the will of the people.

In 1924, Lenin was forced to act so he introduced what he called the New Economic Plan, which involved peasants being allowed a very small plot of land to grow their own food. By the fall of communism in the 1990s, these plots had produced over 50 percent of the foodstuffs in the Soviet Union and were part of a massive "Black Market" economy. Ironically, this market was probably one of the largest and most successful examples of a truly free market economy; that is, with no government interference at all.

Another phenomenon emerged from the imposition of Marx's communist ideology, namely, the elimination of religion and the moral code of Christianity that fed people's souls as food fed their bodies. In most Western nations, this lack of religion associated with the expansion of socialism, combined with

Darwin's evolutionary ideology, eliminated religion. Church attendance continues to be quite high in the US, but churches throughout Europe are almost empty and many closing every month. People were left with a yearning for a moral code. They had a multitude of challenges about their individual needs. They were concerned about their purpose in this life and what came after. These are the questions and issues dealt with in Christianity, that was gradually being eliminated as an option. Socialism and Darwinism suppressed and subjugated the individual to the state. The problem is, as Christianity recognizes, free will was the one feature God provided to distinguish humans from all the other animals. It can be suppressed with great effect and for long periods as totalitarian regimes demonstrate, but the free will constantly and unceasingly strives to be free. The truth is that the very first time Marxism was tried, it failed and has done so on every occasion since.

All these conditions opened the floodgates of another form of tyranny—environmentalism, the new religion for the new age. Vaclav Klaus, former president of the Czech Republic, lived through communism, so he was aware of what was happening. He explained the threat in his 2007 book *Blue Planet in Green Shackles,* saying that, "Nevertheless, there is another threat on the horizon. I see this threat in environmentalism, which is becoming a new dominant ideology, if not a religion. Its main weapon is raising the alarm and predicting the human life-endangering climate change based on man-made global warming."

This threat of global warming was the perfect vehicle for the new form of totalitarianism. It was universal and so required a single world government. It provided a new code in the form of a religion to let the high priests control the moral high ground.

It allowed them to think they could play God and, with their irreligious science and technology, they could control nature. Consider the ludicrous claim that they were going to stop climate change.

How threatening is the religion of environmentalism to God's people? I will explain in this book.

Stalin, directly or indirectly, murdered more people than any political leader in history. But he, like Hitler, took political control. That doesn't make him any less to blame for the deaths, but it does make him more easily linked, identifiable, and therefore accountable. It is entirely possible he never actually killed anyone. Henchmen did the work and they are always available as Machiavelli observed, "One who deceives will always find those who allow themselves to be deceived."

Others have killed people indirectly by implementing ideas, but few understand that there is not a great deal of difference if the ideas that result in killing are predicated on falsehoods. The fact of the matter is, the modern green movement did not spring into worldwide action until Rachel Carson in 1962 published *Silent Spring*, a devastating argument against the reckless use of the pesticides that were wiping out populations of birds, insects, and other animals. *Silent Spring* is touted as the start of public awareness of environmental issues. It influenced people by playing on their fears of the growing use of herbicides and pesticides. Carson determined, with no evidence, that her husband died from cancer due to exposure to DDT. DDT was initially used by the military in WW II to control malaria, typhus, body lice, and bubonic plague. It was also used by farmers on a variety of food crops in the United States and worldwide for pest control purposes. Public concern increased when the false claim of decline in bird populations appeared. They claimed DDT caused birds to produce eggs with thin shells, resulting in infant mortality. No scientific evidence existed, but it pulled on all the emotional strings.

Western environmentalists successfully pushed for a global ban on DDT. As a result, an estimated 90 million people in Africa and Asia died from malaria. Eventually, many African leaders were moved to act. As the *Premium Times* in Nigeria reported on July 17 2013,

> Amidst staggering mortality and morbidity rates due to malaria in the African continent, African Heads of State and Government have adopted the use of dichlorodiphenyltrichloroethane (DDT), a controversial chemical, as the means of eradicating malaria in the continent. This came after several debates which commenced Wednesday July 10 at a meeting of Health Ministers of various African countries; and continued at meetings of Ambassadors and members of the Permanent Representative Council of the African Union on July 12.[2]

These events have all the components of environmentalism as a religion. They also explain how it, and various components like climate change, which is a subset of environmentalism, provide a valuable vehicle for population control. These are the same people who say the world is overpopulated. It is another misdirection created to justify draconian control and the push for population reduction.

Following the publication of *Silent Spring* and books like Paul Ehrlich's *The Population Bomb*, Democratic President Lyndon

---

[2] http://www.premiumtimesng.com/news/141150-african-countries-adopt-controversial-deadly-chemical-ddt-for-malaria-treatment.html.

Johnson joined many other politicians in adding environmental protection to their platforms. Republican Richard Nixon made considerable progress toward incorporating environmental awareness into his administration. Not only did Nixon create the Environmental Protection Agency (EPA), he also signed the National Environmental Policy Act, or NEPA, which required environmental impact assessments for all large-scale federal projects. Ehrlich, Marx, and Engels, combined with rabid, ill-informed, and deliberately distorted environmentalism, couldn't have delivered a better one-two punch to the American ideals of life, liberty, and the pursuit of happiness—and it's all a Big Lie.

CHAPTER 2

THE BIG LIE

"If you tell a big enough lie and tell it frequently enough, it will be believed."

—Adolph Hitler

The Reverend Thomas Robert Malthus was an English scholar who studied the fields of economy and demography. His "An Essay on the Principle of Population" observed that sooner or later, population will be checked by famine and disease. This led to what is known as the "Malthusian catastrophe." Malthus proposed a theory in 1798 that population would grow at a geometric rate while the food supply grows at an arithmetic rate. The theory has been touted as flawed because of the limited factors observed when he developed the law. It does not include factors such as technology, disease, poverty, international conflict, and natural disasters. In a nutshell, Malthus believed that population growth would exceed the food supply. As Paul Johnson explained in his biography of Charles Darwin,

"Malthus's aim was to discourage charity and reform the existing poor laws, which, he argued, encourage the destitute to breed and so aggravated the problem." Malthus's law was nonsense. He did not prove it; he simply stated it.[3]

What strikes one reading Malthus is the lack of hard evidence throughout. Why did this not strike Darwin? Darwin was an atheist and believer in "survival of the fittest" and was an ardent promoter of Malthus. He took a copy of Malthus's "An Essay on the Principle of Population" with him on his voyages to the Galapagos Islands.

Darwin's *Theory of Evolution*, published in 1859, just eleven years after the Marxist Manifesto, provided two critical components of the destruction of Christianity and the emergence of Environmentalism as the new religion. It provided "scientific" justification for the economic and social theories of Marx and others. It also eliminated the need for God to explain human existence and our difference from other animals. This created many changes, but two are of great importance to our argument. First, his theory led to the creation and dominance of the Social Sciences in universities. All the disciplines of the Social Sciences examine humans and their behavior. They became necessary because Darwin had removed God as the explanation for humans and their differences from other animals. Second, it left people, especially the young, with a moral and intellectual vacuum that provided the ideal conditions for a new religion.

An article of faith among the neo-Malthusians and environmentalists is that the world is getting far too crowded and something must be done. Playing straight from Marx's playbook, Paul Ehrlich, a Stanford University professor who has

---

[3] Paul Johnson, *Darwin: Portrait of a Genius,* (New York, NY: Penguin Group, 2012).

long opined that there are far too many people requiring far too many resources and producing far too much pollution, authored best-selling social engineering books, including *The Population Bomb*, which gained him a reputation amongst environmentalists as a prophetic guru.[4] He remains an icon within their movement even though almost all of his predictions were wrong.

Ehrlich's conviction about overpopulation allows him to blame people for most of the world's problems, especially in the environment—there are just too darn many of them. His solution has always been total population reduction and control. Ehrlich's ominous allegations included equating the earth's surplus of people to a cancer that must be eradicated. As he explains, "A cancer is an uncontrolled multiplication of cells; the population explosion is an uncontrolled multiplication of people . . . we must shift our efforts from treatment of the symptoms to the cutting out of the cancer. The operation will demand many apparently brutal and heartless decisions." He is an example of an atheist playing God.

Ehrlich's madness was further revealed in his dictatorial action plan. "Our position requires that we take immediate action at home and promote effective action worldwide . . . we must have population control at home, hopefully through changes in our value system, but by compulsion if voluntary methods fail."[5] Ehrlich argued that population sacrifices must first begin in the US He dismissed the responsibility of the two most populous countries, China and India, from having to adopt the drastic steps he advocated the US must take first. He did this because the US was not only overpopulated, but that population was based on capitalism and using up resources faster than

---

[4] Paul Erlich, *The Population Bomb*, (Cutchogue, NY: Buccaneer Books, 1995).
[5] Ibid.

less developed nations. This idea of setting developed against less developed nations appeared later in the Kyoto Protocol. It penalized only developed nations, with them paying less developed nations to offset the damage the developed nations had done. It was a purely socialistic massive transfer of wealth.

Ehrlich asked if Americans would "be willing to slaughter our dogs and cats in order to divert pet food protein to the starving masses in Asia." One proposal often mentioned by Ehrlich was "the addition of temporary sterilants to water supplies or staple food"[6] in order to achieve a zero population growth. Ehrlich forecasted that one of three scenarios would likely occur—first, there would be global food riots, and war could break out. He cast the US as the worldwide villain because of this country's insistence on using agricultural chemicals that would have been banned by the UN. Second, more than one billion people would die in one year alone because of disease and plague precipitated by overpopulation. Third, people would simply perish due to mass starvation. "Hundreds of millions of people will starve to death" in the 1970s and eighties, he wrote.

Most of the grim results would occur by the 1980s and the calamitous outcome would be determined before the year 2000. After the publication of *The Population Bomb*, Ehrlich made an updated pronouncement that the US population would dwindle to less than 23 million people by 1999.[7]

Ehrlich came up with a new twist to sell his neo-Malthusian snake oil by combining patriotism with the number of children a couple may have. In 2009, he told the *Christian Science Monitor* he wanted patriotic Americans to stop at two as a resolution of the world's biggest problem, overpopulation.

[6] Ibid.
[7] Ibid.

In 1990, Paul Ehrlich revisited old ground with a new release entitled *Population Explosion*. In it, Ehrlich blames virtually every human catastrophe, both real and imagined, on overpopulation and religion. And guess who wrote Ehrlich's dust jacket endorsement—none other than a Tennessee senator named Al Gore. "If every candidate for office would read and understand this book we would all live in a more peaceful and secure world."[8] Al Gore went on to become vice president, with Ehrlich empowered as his trusted advisor, creating a movie about anthropogenic global warming called *An Inconvenient Truth*.

Paul Ehrlich's personal credibility was slightly diminished, but the idea of overpopulation had taken hold. As early as 1994, Ehrlich's predictions were proving wrong, but this did not stop the United Nations, with the enthusiastic support and participation of Al Gore, from holding a population conference in Cairo, Egypt.[9] The conference underscored the falsity of the claims. They ignored the fact that the Netherlands has among the highest population densities but also the highest living standards. The location of the conference was chosen because central Cairo presents the image of beggars, poverty, and population densities. This conference was born out of what had occurred just two years earlier, the 1992 Rio Summit. Information for the Cairo population conference[10] says: "The Rio Declaration on Environment and Development and Agenda 21, adopted by the international community at the United Nations Conference on Environment and Development, calls

---

[8] Paul Ehrlich, Anne Ehrlich, *The Population Explosion*, (Simon & Schuster, 1990).
[9] Source: http://www.ibiblio.org/pub/archives/whitehouse-papers/1994/Sep/1994-09-13-VP-Gore-on-Close-ofPopulation-and-Development-Conf,
[10] The United Nations International Conference on Population and Development (ICPD) held from 5–13 September 1994 in Cairo, Egypt. http://www.iisd.ca/cairo.html.

for patterns of development that reflect the new understanding of these and other intersectoral linkages."[11]

This is how they linked overpopulation, global warming, and all other false environmental catastrophes. As they said, "Explicitly integrating population into economic and development strategies will both speed up the pace of sustainable development and poverty alleviation and contribute to the achievement of population objectives and an improved quality of life of the population."[12]

Al Gore explained in his statement at the Cairo conference:

> No single solution will be sufficient by itself to produce the patterns of change so badly needed. But together, over a sufficient length of time, a broad-based strategy will help us achieve a stabilized population and thereby improve the quality of life for our children. The Program of Action just adopted in Cairo offers us a plan that will work and that has the full support of the United States.[13]

John Holdren, President Obama's handpicked science advisor, was also directly involved in creating the myth of overpopulation. He joined with Ehrlich to co-author *Ecoscience: Population, Resources, and Environment,* which became central to the links between the three issues. In the book, Holdren illustrated the methodology by which the overpopulation issue could be confronted using the US Constitution. Among many proposals for population control he wrote, "Indeed, it has been concluded that compulsory population-control laws, even including laws requiring compulsory abortion, could be

---

[11] http://www.iisd.ca/Cairo/program/p03001.html.
[12] http://www.unfpa.org/pds/sustainability.htm.
[13] http://www.un.org/popin/icpd2.htm.

sustained under the existing Constitution if the population crisis became sufficiently severe to endanger the society."[14]

The trick is that Holdren is the person who decides when the population has reached a crisis level and when it endangers society.

Despite the fact that Gore's movie script is full of errors, the film received an Oscar. Ironically, this is a reasonable award because the movie was produced by Hollywood people and is a superb piece of propaganda.

We know it is propaganda because one week before the movie was awarded a Nobel Peace Prize, a UK court issued a ruling on a case brought against the United Kingdom Department of Education for showing the movie in the classroom. The context of his ruling was this provision of the Education Act. "The context and nub of the dispute are the statutory provisions described in their side headings as respectively relating to 'political indoctrination' and to the 'duty to secure balanced treatment of political issues' in schools." In his ruling Justice Burton wrote,

> I viewed the film at the parties' request. Although I can only express an opinion as a viewer rather than as a judge, it is plainly, as witnessed by the fact that it received an Oscar this year for best documentary film, a powerful, dramatically presented and highly professionally produced film. It is built round the charismatic presence of the ex-Vice President, Al Gore, whose crusade it now is to persuade the world of the dangers of climate change caused by global warming. It is now common ground that it is not simply a science film—although it is clear that it is based substantially on scientific

---

[14] Paul Ehrlich, *Ecoscience: Population, Resources, Environment,* (W. H. Freemen & Co. Ltd, 1978).

research and opinion—but that it is a political film, albeit of course not party political. Its theme is not merely the fact that there is global warming, and that there is a powerful case that such global warming is caused by man, but that urgent, and if necessary expensive and inconvenient, steps must be taken to counter it, many of which are spelt out.[15]

No wonder the public is confused.

Gore continued to elude debate on the topic of global warming and used the Nobel Peace Prize money to fund his PR firm, the Alliance for Climate Protection, conveniently located just down the street from Ehrlich's Stanford campus office. Gore would lend fatherly advice on global warming to Barack Obama, a man steeped in Marxist machinations. Obama pushed an updated version of a cap and trade scheme originally envisioned by Silicon Valley's most prestigious venture capital firms owned by Gore. A critical meeting occurred at the White House in 1997 between Clinton, Gore, and Ken Lay, president of Enron that later collapsed because of wrongdoing, and Lord Browne, CEO of BP, who foundered with the oil leak in the Gulf of Mexico. The meeting set the stage for the entire carbon credit, cap and trade scandal. Gore and his huckster crony proponents of cap and trade were comfortably in place to rake in billions off the scheme. As the *Wall Street Journal* pointed out, the proponents of cap and trade like to pretend that the system is a free market-based scheme, but when it actually provides cheaper fossil fuels, they want government intervention.[16] The global warming fanatics want it both ways on cap and trade, but on both fronts, they fail. They believe that cap and trade is free market, but it isn't;

---

[15] http://www.bailii.org/ew/cases/EWHC/Admin/2007/2288.html.
[16] http://www.wsj.com/articles/climate-of-corruption-1410292196.

and they believe it will make fossil fuels so expensive that the only viable option will be "green" energy, but even that failed miserably. In Europe, where despite green energy polices having been disastrous, they continue to purport that they will succeed if only you make them bigger!

In 2009, the *New York Times* exposed how Al Gore stood to benefit to the tune of billions of dollars if the carbon tax proposals he pushes come to fruition in the United States, and they documented how he had already lined his pockets on the back of exaggerated fear mongering about global warming.[17] The *NY Times*' John M. Broder revealed how one of the companies Gore invested in, Silver Spring Networks, received a contract worth $560 million from the Energy Department to install "smart meters" in people's homes to record and regulate energy usage. The article went on to say that "Kleiner Perkins Caufield & Byers, a venture capital firm located in Silicon Valley and its partners, including Mr. Gore, could recoup their investment many times over in coming years," and Gore is "well positioned to profit from this green transformation, if and when it comes . . . . Gore is poised to become the world's first 'carbon billionaire,'[18] profiteering from government policies he supports that would direct billions of dollars to the business ventures he has invested in," wrote Broder. [19]

Since he left office, Gore's personal net worth has skyrocketed on the back of his global warming alarmism and the financial dividends this has reaped. Gore's assets totaled less than $2 million in 2001, and although he refuses to give a figure for his current net worth, a recent single investment of $35 million in

---

[17] http://www.nytimes.com/2009/11/03/business/energy-environment/03gore.html?_r=0.
[18] Ibid.
[19] Ibid.

Capricorn Investment Group, a private equity fund, illustrates just how fast Gore has enriched himself from his climate change bandwagon.

Al's political friend, Barack Obama, continues to use the EPA to push the climate change bandwagon through cap and trade systems and other anti-fossil fuel policies forced on US states.

In June 2014, Senate Republicans urged President Obama to repeal his packaged scheme to cajole states into imposing cap and trade plans on carbon dioxide emissions. Republicans insisted it would result in higher energy prices and huge job losses as coal-fired power plants and coal mines stood to be shut down by federal emissions reduction compliance mandates.

Despite Obama's failed cap and trade, he kept repackaging the same scheme, trying to get it pushed through either by Congress or by regulatory fiat. That is the Obama way after all—if the democratic process fails to give him what he wants, he simply decrees it by executive order and imposes it on the people, like Benito Mussolini—an imperial dictating despot using strategies right out of the Marxist textbooks. President Obama's handpicked science czar John Holdren let the Marxian cat out of the bag long ago when he wrote up a massive campaign to de-develop the United States.

> Resources must be diverted from frivolous and wasteful uses in overdeveloped countries to filling the genuine needs of underdeveloped countries. This effort must be largely political, especially with regard to our overexploitation of world resources, but the campaign should be strongly supplemented by legal and boycott action against polluters and others whose activities damage the environment. The

need for de-development presents our economists with a major challenge. They must design a stable, low-consumption economy in which there is a much more equitable distribution of wealth than in the present one. Redistribution of wealth both within and among nations is absolutely essential, if a decent life is to be provided for every human being.[20]

On April 22, 2015, in his Earth Day proclamation, Obama said, "Today, our planet faces new challenges, but none pose a greater threat to future generations than climate change." In his proclamation he wrote, "As a Nation, we must act before it is too late."[21] On the heels of his proclamation, John Kerry, in an Earth Day op-ed for USA Today[22], declared that climate change has put America "on a dangerous path—along with the rest of the world." Both Obama and Kerry cited rapidly warming global temperatures and ever-more-severe storms caused by climate change as reasons for urgent action. Just two months before, in February 2015, the UN IPCC's (Intergovernmental Panel on Climate Change) top climate scientist, Rajendra Pachauri, acknowledged inadvertently during his resignation in a farewell letter, "The protection of Planet Earth, the survival of all species and sustainability of our ecosystems is more than a mission. It is my religion and my dharma."[23]

Christiana Figueres, the official leading the UN's effort to forge a new international climate treaty later this year in Paris, told reporters in February that the real goal is "to change the economic development model that has been reigning for

---

[20] http://americaswatchtower.com/2010/09/16/barack-obamas-science-czar-advocates-the-de-development-of-the-united-states/.
[21] http://www.wsj.com/articles/the-climate-change-religion-1429832149.
[22] http://www.usatoday.com/story/opinion/2015/04/21/earth-day-2015-john-kerry-climate-change-column/26070603/.
[23] https://www.ipcc.ch/pdf/ar5/150224_pachauri_letter.pdf.

at least 150 years." Obama pledged his commitment to the United Nations Framework Convention on Climate Change, stating that the commitment would lock the US into reducing greenhouse gas emissions by more than 25 percent by 2025 and "economy-wide emission reductions of 80 percent or more by 2050."[24] Human ecology problems and solutions brought to you by the conjoined Marxist twins—Holdren and Ehrlich, and their unsavory pals.

As you can see, an elite brigade of zealots has cleverly created a new political platform to carry out their collectivist goals—leveling the playing field in the redistribution of wealth and destroying personal liberty by utilizing something that Karl Marx himself never envisioned. Marx would have salivated at the idea of utilizing junk pseudoscience to force you to believe that your lifestyle is responsible for altering the earth's atmosphere. It's all a great big lie, but the end justifies the means—it is the devil's way.

---

[24] http://unfccc.int/files/focus/indc_portal/application/pdf/u_s_cover_note_indc_and_accompanying_information.pdf

CHAPTER 3

THE GOSPEL ACCORDING TO AL GORE

"And thus in the primitive simplicity of their minds and more readily fall victims to the big lie than the small lie."
—Adolf Hitler, *Mein Kampf*

Ehrlich's pal Al Gore joined the AGW (Anthropogenic Global Warming, meaning human-caused global warming) movement in the 1980s. Under the tutoring of NASA scientist James Hansen, Gore became fervently convinced that the only way to preserve humanity from the coming climate catastrophe would be to lead a worldwide campaign to convince individuals, corporations, politicians, and world leaders to drastically curtail the production and use of fossil fuels. Of course doing so would severely reduce our wealth, standard of living, and quality of life.

Another influence was former Senator Timothy Wirth, who was instrumental in finding Hansen and bringing him before a 1998 Senate Committee at which he stated he was 99 percent certain that human CO2 was causing global warming. Wirth's 1993 comment that "We've got to ride the global warming issue. Even if the global warming theory is all wrong, we will be doing the right thing . . ."[25] exposes the fact that they didn't care about the truth. What they wanted was an environmental green vehicle to carry their political agenda of population reduction and total government control. The Canadian Minister of the Environment reiterated the view when she said, "No matter if the science of global warming is all phony—climate change provides the greatest opportunity to bring about justice and equality in the world."[26]

As I alluded to in the previous chapter, Gore's illustrated book titled *An Inconvenient Truth* was followed with a movie of the same title that has already been mentioned and that has been shown around the globe, including to millions of students in classrooms throughout the Western Hemisphere. Gore has trained hundreds of supporters to make his prepared presentation. Gore's partisan ideological book and movie are presented as objective climate science and a moral compass dealing with what he calls the planetary emergency of global warming. His presentation promotes a remarkable number of false and unsupported claims.

In the week Gore received his Nobel Prize, a UK judge ruled that if shown in the schools the teacher must identify nine major scientific errors,[27] as well as the propaganda nature of the work. He also said a balance should be provided by showing a

---

[25] Michael Fumento, *Science Under Siege: Balancing Technology and the Environment,* (New York, NY: William Morrow & Company, 1993), Timothy Wirth quote.

[26] http://www.forbes.com/sites/larrybell/2013/02/05/in-their-own-words-climate-alarmists-debunk-their-science/.

[27] http://www.washingtonpost.com/wp-dyn/content/article/2007/10/11/AR2007101102134.html

countering documentary, such as *The Great Global Warming Swindle*.[28]

Gore's book claims that global warming is endangering the population of polar bears, stating that polar bears have been drowning in significant numbers due to the loss of Arctic sea ice. This assertion was based on nothing more than a single 2005 report that found that four polar bears had drowned in one month due to an exceptional storm with high winds and waves in the Beaufort Sea. The truth is that the polar bear population has risen significantly in the Svalbard Islands and across the Arctic. In Canada, Inuit people report they have never seen so many bears. The only possible threat to polar bears comes from hunting, which involves issuing licenses each year and hunting polar bears is easily controlled and modified annually through legal restrictions on the number of licenses sold. More important, Inuit families were able to sell the license if numbers allowed and, until the US government intervened, doing so was a major source of income.

The major error in all of these claims of collapse of populations and extinctions involves a false premise. It is the same false premise that exists about climate, namely that neither animal populations nor climate changes. Animal populations fluctuate significantly all the time and extinction is the norm. However, consider the fact that it is estimated we have only discovered and identified approximately 35 percent of the species on the planet. Every month many more species are discovered than go extinct. Even the supposedly environmentally aware National Geographic Society had an article in May 2014 listing the "Top 10 New Species of 2014."

---

[28] http://scienceandpublicpolicy.org/monckton/goreerrors.html.

Gore bases all his ideas about climate on what the UN Intergovernmental Panel on Climate Change (IPCC) says. Gore claims the IPCC represents the opinion of the global scientific community and accepts without question that carbon dioxide in the atmosphere is almost the sole cause of runaway global temperatures. According to climatological and geological experts, shifts in CO_2 have no relationship to global warming or climate change. In fact, in every record from any time period in the earth's history, temperature increases *before* CO_2 does. This is in complete contradiction to the IPCC claim that CO_2 increase causes temperature increase. The most fundamental assumption of their claim is absolutely wrong. The only place in the world where CO_2 increases before temperature is in the computer models the IPCC uses to predict global warming. No wonder every prediction they have ever made was wrong.

Consequently, Gore's linking their predictions to any change in CO_2 levels is wrong. The list is long but at the top are his predicted rises in sea levels resulting from an increase in CO_2 levels in the atmosphere. Gore also suggests that an increase of only 100 ppmv of CO_2 in the atmosphere, a rise from 385–485 ppmv, (parts per million by volume), would produce the difference between an Ice Age temperature minimum and interglacial temperature maximum. The CO_2 increase does not produce enough temperature increase to explain the range of temperatures between the Ice Age and now. He ignores the geologic record that shows the Ordovician Ice Age occurring with CO_2 levels of over 4000 ppmv. Gore overstates by ten times the mainstream climate science consensus by exaggerating it with an endless estimate of the effects of rising levels of CO_2 on global temperature and sea level rise. He even disagrees with the

IPCC, who puts the potential rise at a fraction of his claim. Of course, Gore wants the sea levels to rise, which is why he made computer-generated flooding a major part of his movie. He also wants the polar bears to drown to raise the emotional quotient of his alarmist political agenda. Author and one of the most influential and prolific journalists in America in the 1930s, H. L. Mencken, who is described as "a controversialist, humorous journalist, and pungent critic of American life"[29] in the tradition of Mark Twain, explained, "The whole aim of practical politics is to keep the populace alarmed, and hence clamorous to be led to safety, by menacing it with an endless series of hobgoblins, all of them imaginary."

People display their confusion and exploitation in their speeches. Gore refers to carbon dioxide as global warming pollution. The US EPA has officially declared that CO_2 is a harmful substance that should be regulated by the federal government; however, CO_2 is not a pollutant. CO_2 is a vital atmospheric trace gas that is an essential nutrient and food for plant life. Without CO_2, there would be no plants, and therefore no oxygen, without which there would be no animals, including humans. Gore would like you to believe the very thing you exhale is problematic; because you breathe, you are a problem. Gore claims levels are dangerously high when they are at the lowest levels in 300 million years. We also know from research and addition of CO_2 to greenhouses that plants function best at about 1200 ppmv (parts per million by volume). So at current levels of 390 ppmv they are essentially malnourished. President Obama talks about carbon pollution. He thinks he is saying

---

[29] Adam Augustyn Ed, *American Literature from the 1850s to 1945*, (New York, NY: Rosen Publishing Group, 2010), 108.

carbon dioxide pollution, but carbon is a solid while carbon dioxide is a gas. They are not the same thing at all.

Gore has been one of the biggest proponents of the religion of man-made global warming for the last three decades. In the summer of 1992, Al Gore's book *Earth in the Balance* was published, knighting him as the world's foremost global warming go-to-guy and he has worked overtime to convince the world that humans are the single culprit of global warming and latterly climate change. According to Gore, ordinary things such as burning coal, or driving your car to work, or cutting down trees to produce lumber for your home, all have dire consequences. Notice that there is a central assumption to these ideas, namely that human actions are unnatural. The *Greenpeace Report on Global Warming* said carbon dioxide is added to the atmosphere naturally and unnaturally.[30] The unnatural portion is from humans, which implies if human activities are unnatural, humans are unnatural. This is another part of the environmentalist doctrine. Ironically, if we are unnatural, then it implies that God put us here, but they don't complete their thoughts if it contradicts their deceit.

In 1999, Gore founded the Alliance for Climate Protection. In 2004, he and David Blood, formerly the chief executive of Goldman Sachs Asset Management, founded Generation Investment Management (GIM) to manage carbon-trading credits. In 2010, Ameritrade disclosed that GIM raked in a whopping seven billion plus dollars. In addition, Gore generates an average $150,000 per global warming speaking engagement and is still pulling in exorbitant lucre from his inconvenient

---

[30] Jeremy Leggett, *Global Warming: Greenpeace Report,* (New York, NY: Oxford University Press, 1990), 78.

truths, or perhaps more accurately, "convenient lies" mantra. Despite his outlandish claims that sea levels are rising, he bought a deluxe oceanfront property in the San Francisco Bay area.

Gore churns out his deceptive fraud using terms like *artic ice shrinkage, melting polar ice caps, polar bears drowning, drastic species reduction, freak storms, drastic sea levels rising,* and *coral bleaching,* further demonizing CO2 for all of it. Al Gore famously predicted in 2008 that the Arctic would be ice free within five years—so by 2013. It's been seven years since his prediction and the Arctic is still full of ice. In fact, the Arctic did the exact opposite of what Gore predicted and increased 50 percent from 2012 levels.

Coupled with his flagrant hypocrisy, hyperbole, and hysteria, Gore has lined his deep pockets with enormous amounts of money for decades. This unsavory huckster continues his global warming echo chamber rhetoric about a "climate crisis" wherever he goes, yet not one of his preposterous claims has ever proved accurate. Meanwhile, his company, GIM, continues to bring in billions by issuing certificates that enable investors in alternative energy companies to believe they have helped improve the earth's climate by investing in carbon offset arrangements. In doing so, they supposedly offset their enormous carbon footprint created by using private jets and other significant uses of energy. Their investments in renewable energy companies and in developing green energy all serve to demonstrate their commitment to saving the earth. Gore conveniently overlooks the fact that there is an enormous well-funded global warming industry, in which Gore is a significant player. The climate change industry supports the academics, scientists, nongovernmental organizations (NGOs), media, and political groups that together promote the AGW movement. Despite a number of scientists and researchers having disputed the numerous errors in *An Inconvenient Truth*, he still refuses to debate his critics despite many invitations. Instead of debating, he demonizes anyone who dares to disagree with him, calling them "climate deniers" and insisting that these climate criminals should be dealt with in the harshest way. In fact his pal Naomi Oreskes, affiliate Professor of Earth and Planetary Sciences at Harvard University, likes the idea of having climate "deniers" prosecuted under the RICO act (Racketeer Influenced and Corrupt Organizations Act).[31]

The problem is that Gore creates the false fear and then not only profits from it, but also demonizes anyone who dares question him. In addition, his lifestyle is in complete contradiction to his preaching, and he is that most despised of people, a hypocrite.

The sale of carbon credits is the modern equivalent of another religious scam that exploited religion and people's weaknesses, namely, the sale of indulgences during the Middle Ages.

Alexander Cockburn in an article titled, "From Papal Indulgences to Carbon Credits; But Is Global Warming a Sin?" made the comparison between indulgences and carbon credits. He wrote,

> Then as now, a buoyant market throve on fear. The Roman Catholic Church was a bank whose capital was secured by the infinite mercy of Christ, Mary and the Saints, and so the Pope could sell indulgences, like checks. The sinners established a line of credit against bad behavior and could go on sinning.

---

[31] https://www.youtube.com/watch?t=4376&v=CPMDPrGA9ZI (112:00-113:00). http://www.independentsentinel.com/senator-whitehouse-wants-global-warming-deniers-in-prison/.

> Today a world market in "carbon credits" is in formation. Those whose "carbon footprint" is small can sell their surplus carbon credits to others, less virtuous than themselves.[32]

It is a good analogy, but especially so as both create a source of income for those who identify and define the problem, exploit the guilt, and offer a solution. They also do nothing to ameliorate the supposed problems, the amount of sinning or, in Gore's case, the amount of CO_2 going into the atmosphere from human sources. In fact, they almost guarantee an increase in both cases. The analogy fails because sin exists whether it is a transgression against religious or secular law. CO_2 in the atmosphere from any source, including humans, is not causing global warming or climate change. It is essential to life on the planet and it has been demonstrated that an increase in atmospheric levels is beneficial to distribution, abundance, and productivity.

There is pathetic irony in the fact that financial gain, if not necessarily the underlying motive, is certainly the reward of these modern day gangsters. Financial gain is one of the unforgivable sins of the evil energy companies producing the planet-destroying CO_2.

An Inconvenient Truth is full of "thick and fast" examples. Gore's public appearances are a litany of stories from the past designed to capture through fear and to stick in the mind. The media repeats and amplifies them.

Gore was involved early in the establishment of carbon credits as a key part of the Kyoto Accord. Even though the Accord has failed, carbon credits, its most bizarre by-product, survived in the form of carbon taxes. The latest efforts scheduled

---

[32] http://www.counterpunch.org/2007/04/28/is-global-warming-a-sin/.

for Paris in September 2015 will see attempts to expand carbon credits through the "Green Fund" managed by the UN to fund global governance.

Another person who benefited from the global warming scare and the sale of carbon credits was Maurice Strong, who as I will explain later, was the central figure at the UN, founder of the United Nations Environment Program (UNEP) and the Intergovernmental Panel on Climate Change, and a very good friend of Al Gore.

Here is what James Murray wrote about Gore's behavior.

Apparently rather than debating the merits of his argument in a rational and reasoned manner, Gore is left only with ad hominem attacks and smug condescension toward his critics. Self-avowed "P.R. agent for the planet" Al Gore says those who still doubt that global warming is caused by man—among them, Vice President Dick Cheney—are acting like the fringe groups who think the 1969 moon landing never really happened, or who once believed the world is flat.[33]

What is Al Gore's story? Here is what he told Congress in March 2007 in a presentation that broke their rules of having submitted a presentation in advance and leaving before answering questions.

"The science is settled," Gore told the lawmakers. Carbon dioxide emissions—from cars, power plants, buildings, and other sources—are heating the earth's atmosphere." He reiterated the same 'science is settled' mantra on the David Lettermen Show.[34]

---

[33] http://usatoday30.usatoday.com/news/mmemmottpdf/gore-on-60-minutes-3-27-2008.pdf, accessed.
[34] https://www.youtube.com/watch?v=w7uGRvwU0CA (43 seconds).

"The planet has a fever," Gore said. "If your baby has a fever, you go to the doctor. If the doctor says you need to intervene here, you don't say, 'Well, I read a science-fiction novel that tells me it's not a problem.'"[35] Gore said that if left unchecked, global warming could lead to a drastic change in the weather, sea levels, and other aspects of the environment.

He raised the threat in 2008 using James Hansen's claim of a "tipping point" in ten years as the basis for arguing that the US has only ten years to become carbon independent.

Gore's objective is to eliminate human production of CO_2 to save people, especially those in developing nations, from dying in severe weather, drowning in rising seas, or starving because of high temperatures and drought. Ironically, instead of increasing the standard of living throughout the world, these policies have resulted in higher energy costs and have lowered the standard of living throughout the world.

The week after Gore's film won an Academy Award, the Tennessee Center for Policy Research revealed that Gore's upscale Nashville mansion consumed more electricity in one month than the average household uses in one year. His carbon footprint exceeded the average by a factor of twenty, in other words Gore's Nashville home uses twenty times the electricity of an average US household. A year later, apparently after taking steps to make his home more energy-efficient; his energy use was up 10 percent. Drew Johnson, president of the Tennessee Center said, "Al Gore is a hypocrite and a fraud when it comes to his commitment to the environment, judging by his home energy consumption." In an interview with Jimmy Fallon, late night TV talk show host, Gore said, "This is no longer climate change,

---

[35] http://www.npr.org/templates/story/story.php?storyId=9047642.

we don't call it that, nor do we call it climate disruption as some were calling it—we need to call it what it is—This is a climate catastrophe!" Gore went on to spout bogus nonsensical statistics and concluded his interview by saying, "What we need is a strict planetary regime and tough sanctions on non-compliance, and we are working to bring that about."

Since when did Al Gore become a climatologist? Or better yet when did he become the head of the eco-gestapo? The fact that the planet has been cooling for eighteen years doesn't deter Gore. Gore continues to spew out his ever-mounting warming hysteria, with wilder and more outlandish claims at every interval. The only thing that is full of hot air seems to be him.

CHAPTER 4

Is the Science Settled or Unsettling?

"When a politician . . . says 'the debate is over,' you can be sure of two things: the debate is raging; and he's losing it."

—George Will

"The science is settled. The debate is over." Those were the words of Al Gore (CNN, January 2007) and again in the US Senate hearings in 2008. The claim is so wrong that even some of the mainstream media and many people were perplexed. They know science is an ongoing search. Despite his error, the words bounced around the media echo chamber time and time again. They achieved the goal of getting the first headline, which is the objective. People like Gore know that attempts to correct the record or any further explanation get no attention, yet ironically there has never been a debate, despite ubiquitous pleas from real climatologists and a few politicians. Gore eludes debates by claiming the "science is settled."

The most damming crack in the foundation of anthropogenic (or manmade) global warming, the hypothesis or scientific speculation that human CO2 was causing global warming, occurred in November 2009. Just prior to a major climate conference in Copenhagen at which a global carbon tax was to be determined, a thousand e-mails were leaked from an internal computer system within the Climate Research Unit (CRU) at the University of East Anglia (UEA) in the UK. Journalist and author James Delingpole dubbed it "Climategate"[36] because it mirrored the revelations of wrongdoing in the Watergate debacle. What they revealed was how a small group of highly influential British and US scientists had for years been secretly discussing ways in which the research could be manipulated to make their case for human-caused climate change. The once highly regarded CRU's credibility was reduced to junk science through the revelation of the damming e-mail exchanges. The e-mails revealed that the world's leading climate scientists were working in cahoots to block freedom of information requests to review their data, thus marginalizing dissenting scientists. They manipulated peer-reviewed processes and even deleted inconvenient temperature readings, manipulating the data until it reflected what they wanted. They wrote computer programs to make their climate models produce the results to support their claims. George Monbiot, a reporter for the left-wing UK newspaper *The Guardian* and a strong supporter of global warming and the CRU, was shaken to the core. As he wrote,

It's no use pretending that this isn't a major blow. The e-mails extracted by a hacker from the climatic research unit at the

---

[36] http://blogs.telegraph.co.uk/news/jamesdelingpole/100018246/climategate-how-the-greatest-scientific-scandal-of-our-generation-got-its-name/.

University of East Anglia could scarcely be more damaging. I am now convinced that they are genuine, and I'm dismayed and deeply shaken by them.[37]

Why would they do this? The simple answer seems to be—just follow the money—after all, that model seems to work pretty well for the former vice president. Money and career advancement are motivating factors to fudge data. The money, especially government funding and huge grant infusions, were used to buy off scientists and others who would provide the "settled science" they needed. Let's consider the financial issues first, but the ultimate reason among the few at the top is power. Gore has made a great deal of money; however, his original involvement was the need for a vehicle to advance his political career. It is interesting that in his introduction, Gore speaks about how reading Rachel Carson's *Silent Spring* (1962) when he was fourteen years old shocked him into environmental awareness, which developed further during his studies with pioneering scientist Dr. Roger Revelle at Harvard.[38]

From the financial and career rewards perspective, consider Phil Jones, director of the CRU. Jones was the recipient of roughly $19 million in research grants. Jones knew what they were doing was wrong because he sent e-mails to other CRU people, urging them to erase e-mails and explaining how to avoid Freedom of Information (FOI) requests. In 2005 he wrote;

Just sent loads of station data to Scott. Make sure he documents everything better this time! And don't leave stuff lying around on ftp sites - you never know who is trawling

[37] http://www.monbiot.com/2009/11/23/the-knights-carbonic/.
[38] Al Gore, *AN Inconvenient Truth, The Crisis of Global Warming,* (New York, NY: Viking Books for Young Readers, 2007).

them. The two MMs have been after the CRU station data for years. If they ever hear there is a Freedom of Information Act now in the UK, I think I'll delete the file rather than send to anyone. Does your similar act in the US force you to respond to enquiries within 20 days? Ours does! The UK works on precedents, so the first request will test it. We also have a data protection act, which I will hide behind. Tom Wigley has sent me a worried e-mail when he heard about it - thought people could ask him for his model code. He has retired officially from UEA so he can hide behind that. IPR should be relevant here, but I can see me getting into an argument with someone at UEA who'll say we must adhere to it![39]

People at the CRU held lead author positions on critical chapters of the IPCC reports. They effectively controlled the entire process, so exposure of their activities was a serious blow. There is no point in detailing all the transgressions revealed in the e-mails, except to identify specific actions to produce material to support their claim that human CO_2 was causing global warming and temperatures were higher than they had ever been. A graph in the first IPCC report caused a great deal of trouble. The three problems it created were:

- The Medieval Warm Period (MWP) contradicted their claim that the twentieth century was the warmest ever.
- The Little Ice Age (LIA), a cold period from AD 1500 to 1850, showed that the present warming trend began prior to the major impact of the Industrial Revolution. Significant production of CO_2 by humans began only after World War II.

---

[39] http://www.wsj.com/articles/SB10001424052748704779704574553652849094482.

- The trend of the warming since circa 1650 AD was well within natural variability.

In one e-mail, Michael Mann tells Jones it would be nice to "contain the putative" (supposed) Medieval Warm Period (MWP). In testimony before the US Congress, Professor David Deming reported receiving an e-mail from a CRU member who thought he was part of the subterfuge to pursue what the e-mails refer to as "the cause." It bluntly said, "We have to get rid of the Medieval Warm Period."[40]

Michael Mann had developed a technique using tree rings to eliminate the MWP. He was co-opted by the IPCC shortly after getting his PhD and, despite having little experience, became a lead author in the 2001 IPCC Report. It was a meteoric rise. Mann used a selected set of tree rings dominated by one in particular, Bristle Cone Pine, that was deemed unusable, to make a computer model. He ignored the fact that tree rings reflect precipitation patterns, not temperature. As they ran their computer models with tree rings, they showed the "temperature" declining in the twentieth century. So the method eliminated the MWP, but it showed the exact opposite of what they wanted for the twentieth century.

No problem—they simply programmed the computer model to graft on, in a totally unacceptable scientific technique, the modern temperature record. Through stupefying number-crunching mathematical wizardry, Michael Mann meticulously manipulated the data. The result? A bogus graph that looked like a hockey stick positioned horizontally, with the blade protruding straight up. The technique was referred to in the leaked e-mails as

---

[40] https://www.youtube.com/watch?v=u1rj00Boltw (1Minute -23 seconds).

"Mike's Nature trick" after the use of it in the original article in the journal *Nature*, and published in *Geology Research Letters*. Phil Jones produced the blade data that claimed global temperatures had increased 0.6°C in approximately 120 years. He claimed, incorrectly, that this was greater than could occur naturally. What people didn't understand was that he also provided the lie to that claim because the error range was ±0.2°C, or ±33 percent. To put this in context, consider a political poll saying its results were accurate to ±33 percent.

Mann's infamous "the hockey stick" climate model became a popular and devious device to convince the uninformed observer that the earth was undergoing an unprecedented fever. It was like manna from heaven for Al Gore and his carbon credit touting, sky is falling, give us the money and power to save you, pals.

A major test of new scientific research is the ability of other scientists to replicate or reproduce the results—it is called reproducible results. Steve McIntyre and Ross McKitrick tried to replicate this now most famous of all climatological reconstructions, aka Mann's hockey stick, and were stonewalled in obtaining Mann's original data. They were able to recreate enough to discover that Mann's graph relied on a computer algorithm so skewed that it would produce the "hockey stick" more than 99 percent of the time regardless of the data you fed into it. In other words, even though it was comprehensively debunked, Mann's corrupted graph was used in Gore's movie to scare and mislead politicians, a majority of the public, and worst of all, school children. It became the poster child for global warming. It continues to be hailed by global warming advocates as the gospel. The United Nations still carries the stick to compel global policy and Al Gore carries it all the way to the bank.

Both Mann and Jones consistently refused to release their original data. Mann refused to provide his data and then got a court to say it was his intellectual property, even though the taxpayer paid for his research and the results were used for public policy. When Australian scientist Warwick Hughes asked Phil Jones for his data, he replied, "We have 25 years or so invested in the work. Why should I make the data available to you, when your aim is to try and find something wrong with it?"[41] He subsequently reported that the original data was lost. Like Mann and his hockey stick model, the handful of experts from the IPCC and CRU entrusted with monitoring the planet's temperature are agenda-driven and constantly adjusting the records by lowering the historic record to make the rate of warming appear greater.

Gavin Schmidt was a graduate and then on staff at the CRU but is now in control of the influential NASA Goddard Institute for Space Studies (GISS) temperature record. Recently, he held a press conference claiming that 2014 was the warmest year on record. Although it was in his personal briefing notes, he neglected to tell the media that he was only 38 percent sure of his data.[42] Other estimates of global temperature, such as the satellite record from the University of Alabama at Huntsville, showed it was not the warmest year on record. However, Schmidt had the headline and it gave backing to Al Gore's claim that, "the Great Goddess Gaia has a fever."

James Hansen, the director of NASA GISS (National Aeronautics and Space Administration Goddard Institute for Space Studies) for nearly thirty years, is a zealous promoter of

---

[41] Patrick Michaels, *Climate of Extremes: Global Warming Science They Don't Want You to Know,* (Washington. D.C.: Cato Institute, 2010), 66.
[42] http://www.dailymail.co.uk/news/article-2915061/Nasa-climate-scientists-said-2014-warmest-year-record-38-sure-right.html.

global warming since the eighties. Hansen possesses an insatiable appetite for media attention, constantly pushing his personal agenda in a bureaucratic position that requires objectivity. A slick marketer with a penchant for outlandish claims and histrionics, including being arrested in a protest outside the White House, Hansen somehow avoided being prosecuted under the Hatch Act that limits bureaucratic political activities. He became central to the deception about global warming when he took it from behind the scenes of the UN bureaucratic machinations into the public spotlight. Hansen even agreed to an interview on a rooftop in downtown San Francisco conducted by a counterculture Internet-based outfit called TUC radio, during which Hansen hardly sounded like an honorable director of the US government agency but rather more like a Marxist community agitator.[43]

His June 1988 appearance before a US Senate committee, at which he lamented that he was certain that man was the culprit and human CO2 caused global warming, put the entire issue onto the world stage. Coordinators of the drama were Al Gore and former United States Senator Timothy Wirth, although recently John Kerry falsely claimed a role. In a 2007 PBS *Frontline* documentary, Wirth said, "We knew there was this scientist at NASA who had really identified the human impact before anyone else and would testify emphatically at the Gore committee that human CO2 was causing unstoppable global warming."[44] Wirth acknowledged that they had identified the pre-forecasted hottest day of the year in Washington and scheduled the hearing for that day. They went into the hearing

---

[43] Brian Sussman, Climategate: *A Veteran Meterologist Exposes the Global Warming Scam*, (Los Angeles, CA: WND Books, 2010), 47–48.

[44] http://www.pbs.org/wgbh/pages/frontline/hotpolitics/etc/script.html.

room the night before to open the windows and turn off the air conditioning.

"I tell young people that they better start to act up because they're the ones who will suffer," Hansen said. Hansen usually failed to mention that he should have made it clear that all his comments were his own and not his as representative of NASA. Indeed, a characteristic of his career was that he spoke as director of NASA GISS when it suited him and a citizen when that was beneficial. As NASA director, his role should have been collecting data like a scientist—truthfully—and sharing the data, not producing results to influence policy legislation and encourage riots. In February 2009, Hansen wrote an op-ed in the *London Observer* recklessly claiming, "Coal-fired power stations are death factories."[45] Hansen was challenged about abusing the public trust and his agitator antics, including participating in a public protest outside the White House and giving evidence on behalf of Greenpeace activists who bombed a coal plant in England. All this is in contradiction to the political activity limitations put on him as a federal employee under the Hatch Act. He went on the offensive and claimed political interference from the Bush White House. His boss at NASA GISS waited until he was retired to say publicly that the interference did not happen.

The Heinz foundation awarded (rewarded) Hansen with $250,000 for helping make global warming a household phrase. It is also reported that Hansen is said to have acted as a paid consultant to Al Gore during the making of his sci-fi global warming propaganda film. It's ritzy vacations and big money pay-offs when you jump into bed with the big eco fraud. Gore and Hansen led the ignorant to believe that this was the hottest

---

[45] http://www.theguardian.com/commentisfree/2009/feb/15/james-hansen-power-plants-coal.

weather ever, blaming it all on the rampant production of carbon dioxide caused by man's insatiable appetite for fossil fuels.

The truth that you must realize is that CO_2 only accounts for less than 1 percent of the gases in earth's atmosphere, less than 4 percent of the so-called greenhouse gases, and of that sliver only 3 percent is created through anthropogenic (man-made) means. Carbon dioxide has been steadily increasing at a snail's pace since the end of the little Ice Age, but at less than 4 percent, it is at the lowest level in 300 million years. The warming mantra is pure chicanery. How do their mindless ramblings explain the hottest weather ever recorded back in the 1930s when CO_2 levels from fossil fuels were immeasurable? According to the US National Climatic Data Center, 1936 was the hottest overall summer on record in the continental United States.

Despite the facts, temperature keeper James Hansen continued to ignore them and claim to the press that "we only have four years left!" Perhaps he means they only have four more years to dupe the public, so that he and Gore can make even more money and gain greater power. It is interesting that Wirth retired early from the Senate and took a senior position at the UN, likely under the influence of Ted Turner, who had donated one billion dollars to that agency.

The one theme Gore pushed in his movie was that sea levels would rise as Arctic ice melted. Hollywood produced computer images of Florida and New York City under water. He carried out the usual emotional trick of claiming polar bears would drown if they didn't starve to death because the seals were gone. There are so many things wrong with these claims that it would require a complete book to identify and explain them.

As usual, none of these facts stopped the juggernaut of global warming alarmism. In 2005, the United Nations

Environment Program (UNEP) warned that imminent sea-level rise, increasing numbers and intensities of hurricanes, coupled with desertification caused by "man-made global warming" would lead to massive population disruptions. In a handy map, the organization highlighted areas that were supposed to be particularly vulnerable in terms of producing "climate refugees." Especially at risk were regions such as the Caribbean and low-lying Pacific islands, along with coastal areas.

The 2005 UNEP predictions claimed that by 2010, some 50 million "climate refugees" would be frantically fleeing from those regions of the globe. However, not only did the areas in question fail to produce a single "climate refugee,"[46] by 2010, population levels for those regions were actually still soaring. In many cases, the areas that were supposed to be producing waves of "climate refugees" due to land becoming uninhabitable turned out to be some of the fastest-growing places on earth. The only refugees of significance are those fleeing religious persecution in the Middle East or sponsored by Obama administration policies on immigration.

In the Bahamas, for example, according to the 2010 census, there was a major increase in population, going from around 300,000 in 2000 to more than 350,000 by 2010. The population of St. Lucia, meanwhile, grew by 5 percent during the same period. The Seychelles grew by about 10 percent. The Solomon Islands also witnessed a major population boom during that time frame, gaining another 100,000 people, or an increase of about 25 percent.

In China, meanwhile, the top six fastest-growing cities were all within the areas highlighted by the UN as likely sources of

---

[46] http://wattsupwiththat.com/2011/04/15/the-un-disappears-50-million-climate-refugees-then-botches-the-disappearing-attempt/.

"climate refugees." Many of the fastest-growing US cities were also within or close to "climate refugee" danger zones touted by the UN.

Rather than apologizing for its undisputable mistake after being first exposed by reporter Gavin Atkins at Asian Correspondent, the global body responded in typical alarmist fashion: with an Orwellian cover-up seeking to erase all evidence of its ridiculous predictions. First, the UNEP took its "climate refugees" map down from the Web. That failed, of course, because the content was archived online prior to its disappearance down the UN "memory hole."

Then the UNEP tried and failed to distance itself from the outlandish claims, despite the fact that the map was created by a UNEP cartographer, released by UNEP, and repeatedly hyped by the outfit in its scaremongering campaigns. Eventually, as more and more media around the world began picking up the story, a spokesperson for the UN agency claimed the map was removed because it was "causing confusion."

It was hardly the first time UN bureaucrats had made such dire predictions, only to be proven wrong. On June 30, 1989, the Associated Press ran an article headlined, "UN Official Predicts Disaster, Says Greenhouse Effect Could Wipe Some Nations Off Map."[47] In the piece, the director of the UNEP's New York office was quoted as claiming that "entire nations could be wiped off the face of the earth by rising sea levels if global warming is not reversed by the year 2000." He also predicted "coastal flooding and crop failures" that "would create an exodus of 'eco-refugees,'—threatening political chaos."

Other UN predictions were so ridiculous that they were retracted before they could even be proven wrong. Consider,

---

[47] http://wattsupwiththat.com/2014/04/02/the-big-list-of-failed-climate-predictions/, # 85.

as just one example, the scandal that came to be known as "Glaciergate." In its final 2007 report, widely considered the "gospel" of "settled" climate "science," the UN IPCC suggested that Himalayan glaciers could melt by 2035 or sooner. It turns out the wild assertion was lifted from World Wildlife Fund propaganda literature. The IPCC recanted the claim after initially defending it. They should recant almost all their claims because they are without scientific justification, turning lies into truth and altering the past. "Who controls the past controls the future; who controls the present controls the past" from George Orwell in his book *1984*.

CHAPTER 5

INTERGOVERNMENTAL PANEL OF CLIMATE CROOKS

A very effective way of winning a debate or proving a point is to use the words and ideas of the opponent. In the 2001 Intergovernmental Panel on Climate Change (IPCC) Report they say, "In climate research and modeling, we should recognize that we are dealing with a coupled non-linear chaotic system, and therefore that the long-term prediction of future climate states is not possible."[48]

The Intergovernmental Panel on Climate Change (IPCC) is a scientific intergovernmental body under the auspices of the United Nations established in 1988 by two United Nations organizations, the World Meteorological Organization (WMO) and the United Nations Environment Programme (UNEP). It was later endorsed by the United Nations General Assembly through a resolution. The IPCC was chaired by recently retired Rajendra K. Pachauri, a railway engineer who exemplified the

---

[48] http://www.ipcc.ch/ipccreports/tar/wg1/505.htm (paragraph 5).

religious zeal of many controlling the IPCC when he said, "It is my religion."[49]

The IPCC produces reports that support the United Nations Framework Convention on Climate Change (UNFCCC), which is the main international treaty on climate change. The ultimate objective of the UNFCCC, according to their website, is to tackle the challenge of climate change. It states that the Convention's ultimate objective is "stabilization of greenhouse gas concentrations in the atmosphere at a level that would prevent dangerous anthropogenic interference with the climate system."[50] The IPCC claims that their role is to "assess on a comprehensive, objective, open and transparent basis the scientific, technical and socio-economic information relevant to understanding the scientific basis of risk of human-induced climate change, its potential impacts and options for adaptation and mitigation. Review by experts and governments are an essential part of the IPCC process. The Panel does not conduct new research, monitor climate-related data or recommend policies."[51] This was achieved in the standard method by which politicians create the illusion of an independent apolitical investigation that will produce a predetermined result. They determine the definitions and thereby the limits of the investigation. This practice results in most "conspiracy theory" debates, because it is what the politicians ignore that reveals the truth.

The goal was to isolate human CO2 as the cause of global warming. This was done through a very narrow definition of climate change approved by the United Nations Framework Convention on Climate Change (UNFCCC). Article 1 of the

[49] https://www.ipcc.ch/pdf/ar5/150224_pachauri_letter.pdf.
[50] http://unfccc.int/ghg_data/items/3800.php.
[51] https://www.ipcc.ch/pdf/10th-anniversary/anniversary-brochure.pdf.

UNFCCC, a treaty formalized at the "Earth Summit" in Rio in 1992, defined Climate Change as: "a change of climate which is attributed directly or indirectly to human activity that alters the composition of the global atmosphere and which is in addition to natural climate variability observed over considerable time periods."[52]

The problem with this definition is that you cannot determine the human effects if you don't understand the extent and mechanisms of natural variability.

The IPCC does not carry out its own original research, nor does it do the work of monitoring climate or climate-related phenomena itself. The IPCC bases its assessment on so-called published literature, which, despite their claims of purity, includes non-peer-reviewed sources. Supposed experts are asked to write reports, which are then reviewed by governments. The IPCC presents itself as an internationally accepted authority on climate change and produces reports based on a consensus of what are called Working Groups. The entire structure is truly incestuous and all designed to produce the science necessary to support the political objective. Working Group I (WGI) produces the Physical Science Basis report. In order to prevent any drift from the intended message, each report is built on the preceding structure. It is similar to the learning progression of a scientific discipline. You begin with fundamental assumptions that you do not allow to change. WGI is set up to prove that an increase in CO_2 causes an increase in temperature, but every record shows exactly the opposite. The first and most important example occurred after the Antarctic ice cores, which showed temperature and CO_2 variations over 420,000 years, was

---

[52] http://www.unep.org/ieacp/files/pdf/ClimateChange_Manual_Final.pdf.

published in 1991. Just five years later, more detailed analysis showed that throughout the entire record, temperature increased before CO2, not the reverse as initially claimed.

The findings of WGI are taken as the basis for the work of WGII, which produces the Impacts, Adaptation and Vulnerability Report. WGIII starts with the same assumption and produces the Mitigation of Climate Change report. The reports of WGII and III are the source of all alarmism and impending doom, but they only consider the costs of warming, never the benefits.

Mary McCarthy, author and political activist, said, "Bureaucracy, the rule of no one, has become the modern form of despotism."[53] Establishment of the IPCC through the WMO meant total bureaucratic control of every national weather agency. This put control of climate in the hands of the bureaucrats and they in turn controlled the politicians. "In the battle for proper climate science free from politics, there are two levels at which it is the modern form of despotism. In all countries it is in departments of meteorology, weather, climate, or environment. At the global level it is in the United Nations. Regardless of location it is essentially unaccountable and represents the enemy within," McCarthy said.

Instead of working for the people by being apolitical and identifying all sides of an issue so people and politicians can make informed decisions, those selling the global warming fraud have pushed an unproven hypothesis and defended it, even in the face of contradictory evidence. As a result, governments everywhere are introducing or entertaining completely wrong policies. A perfect example of the pervasiveness of climate-based

---

[53] https://en.wikiquote.org/wiki/Bureaucracy.

policy across all parts of society is cap and trade in the Obama stimulus package and budget. "Most of the 2500 members of the Intergovernmental Panel on Climate Change (IPCC) are bureaucrats appointed by their governments to push a political agenda. As MIT professor Richard Lindzen, former member of the IPCC, said, "It is no small matter that routine weather service functionaries from New Zealand to Tanzania are referred to as 'the world's leading climate scientists.' It should come as no surprise that they will be determinedly supportive of the process."[54]

Bureaucratic involvement and actions identify the dilemmas politicians face when confronted with the climate issue. As global warming became the holy grail of the new religion of environmentalism, extremists made it political suicide to ask questions that could be interpreted as showing you did not care about the environment. Second, almost none of them understood science, let alone climate science. When a bureaucrat/scientist convinced politicians they had to adopt policies to stop global warming, they were not in a position to question. Either they didn't know the right questions to ask or they were challenged to explain how they were qualified to challenge a scientist on the subject. A third technique, employed by Hansen when he accused the Bush White House of trying to silence him, was to claim political interference if anyone dared to question.

The IPCC report's first table of figures, inserted by the IPCC's bureaucrats after the scientists had finalized the draft and without their consent, listed four contributions to sea-level rise. The bureaucrats had multiplied the effect of melting ice from the Greenland and West Antarctic Ice Sheets by ten.

---

[54] http://news.heartland.org/newspaper-article/2001/06/01/ipcc-report-criticized-one-its-lead-authors

Of course, the downside is that once the bureaucrats have convinced the politicians, they are on a treadmill. They have to perpetuate the myth that CO2 and especially human CO2 is causing warming. The numbers of ways data are "adjusted" are well documented on Anthony Watts' web site.[55]

Now some are facing the reality of misleading the public as weather continues to confound the computer predictions and the people increasingly ridicule ridiculously wrong forecasts.

Mary McCarthy's comment about bureaucratic despotism is manifest in the exploitation of global warming. Maurice Strong and his appointed bureaucrats at the UN combined with selected national bureaucrats to achieve their political goal as defined by Richard Lindzen. Alfred P. Sloan, professor of meteorology at MIT, said, "Controlling carbon is a bureaucrat's dream. If you control carbon, you control life. Global warming was never about the environment, but about power. Regulating carbon emissions and imposing draconian standards on businesses and personal behavior gives the federal government and global elite's almost unlimited power."

IPCC's chief charlatan Pachauri admitted in the *Times of India* (3 Sept. 2010) that the IPCC reports are merely "compliant politically commissioned work."

> Let's face it, we are an intergovernmental body and our strength and acceptability of what we produce is largely because we are owned by governments. If that was not the case, then we would be like any other scientific body that maybe producing first-rate reports but don't see the light of the day because they don't matter in policy-making. Now clearly, if it's an intergovernmental body and we want

---

[55] http://wattsupwiththat.com.

government's ownership of what we produce, obviously they will give us guidance of what direction to follow, what are the questions they want answered.

There is no evidence for the IPCC's claims of global warming. Besides, as stated earlier their quote indicates that a forecast of the climate is not possible. The truth is that there has been no global warming since 1998—despite the fact that NASA GISS was repeatedly caught red-handed in forging global temperatures; despite the Climate Gate, the IPCC World Gate, the Amazon Gate, the Himalaya Gate scandals and even more; despite the fact that about 700 protesting independent climate scientists call the CO2 preaching the biggest scandal in the history of science. Nevertheless, these charlatans are working harder and harder to reduce emissions of "the gas of life," CO2, which the US Environmental Protection Agency (EPA) has designated a "harmful substance."

Using administrative law, the EPA got the US Supreme Court to classify CO2 under EPA regulatory jurisdiction as a pollutant under the Clean Air Act, using slick phrasing such as "greenhouse gases are pollutants that could endanger human health and welfare." The EPA essentially over-rode a Bush-era decision to allow public comment on the threat of global warming-related pollution. In a December 2009 press release the EPA stated, "Science overwhelmingly shows greenhouse gas concentrations at unprecedented levels due to human activity," and "GHGs are the primary driver of climate change." When the Environmental Protection Agency (EPA) issued the initial endangerment finding in April, administrator Jackson noted that the agency "relied heavily upon the major findings and conclusions from recent assessments of the US Climate Change

Science Program and the Intergovernmental Panel on Climate Change [IPPC]."

Not only does Climategate (the leaked e-mails) seriously call this into question but so do the 700-plus dissenting scientists refuting claims made by the IPCC report. That 700 figure is more than thirteen times the number of scientists (was actually fifty-one) that had a direct role in the IPCC report.

In addition, the IPCC fails to provide accurate information in its reports and also fails to follow scientific methodology. It requires that a hypothesis, an academic word for speculation, is built on certain assumptions and, when proposed, is challenged by other scientists acting in their proper role of skeptics. They try to disprove the hypothesis, a method Karl Popper defined as the process of falsifiability. IPCC worked to prove its hypothesis and branded as skeptics and deniers those who try to practice proper science. Both these labels underscore the fallacy of IPCC's work. All scientists are skeptics and anybody who knows anything about climate knows that climate changes all the time.

The IPCC hypothesis claims human industrial activities are causing runaway global warming, generally called the anthropogenic global warming hypothesis (AGW). Like all hypotheses, it is only as valid as the assumptions on which it is based. They are as follows:

CO_2 is a gas that traps heat in the atmosphere, a so-called greenhouse gas.

If CO_2 levels increase, global temperature will increase.

CO_2 levels will increase because of continued increasing human population growth and expanding industrialization.

The second assumption is central to the hypothesis. The problem is that in every record of any duration for any time period, the temperature increases before CO_2 increases. This is in complete and absolute contradiction and alone destroys their claims. It also explains why their climate predictions are always wrong. They were wrong from the start, but instead of re-examining the science, they started calling them "projections" and producing a range of forecasts. Even the lowest "projections" are wrong. The only place in the world where a CO_2 increase precedes a temperature increase is in the IPCC computer models.

Gore claims his research is based on the IPCC reports, particularly the 2001 report, including the hockey stick. His movie, *An Inconvenient Truth,* was the most successful use of the media to determine the public view of the false information of the IPCC.

The entire tone of the climate debate was established by one of Al Gore's pals, the late Stanford climatologist Stephen Schneider, who said in a 1989 interview with *Discover* magazine:

> On the one hand we are ethically bound to the scientific method, in effect promising to tell the truth, the whole truth, and nothing but, which means that we must include all the doubts, caveats, ifs and buts. On the other hand, we are not just scientists, but human beings as well. And like most people, we'd like to see the world a better place, which in this context translates into our working to reduce the risk of potentially disastrous climate change. To do that we have to get some broad-based support, to capture the public's imagination. That, of course, entails getting loads of media coverage. So we have to offer up scary scenarios, make simplified, dramatic statements, and make little mention of any doubts we might have. This double ethical bind which we frequently find ourselves in cannot be solved by any

formula. Each of us has to decide what the right balance is between being effective and being honest. I hope that means being both.

And there is the fundamental difference between a Christian view and the amoral, political scientific view. There is no balance between "being effective and being honest." For Schneider, Gore, and all the other proponents of human-induced global warming, the end justifies the means. If you have to lie, then it is justified to "save the planet."

No, the earth is not warming, as Al Gore and his globalist pals would like you to believe. In fact, it's in an eighteen year cooling trend that is simply not supposed to happen according to IPCC science. Their predictions were completely wrong and that means the science of the IPCC is wrong. Proper science requires you reconsider the science, but the IPCC and Gore chose to change the titles. Global Warming became Climate Change, and now as is touted by John Holdren, Climate Disruption.

Scientists at the Climatic Research Unit (CRU) knew they had a problem. Thomas Huxley had identified it over a century earlier: "The great tragedy of science—the slaying of a beautiful hypothesis by an ugly fact."

The ugly fact developed after 1998. CO_2 levels continued to increase, but temperature stopped increasing, in contradiction to their major assumption. One of the leaked e-mails from the Minns/Tyndall Centre on the UEA campus identified the CRU scientists' reactions. Nick Campbell, former United Nations Environment Programme co-chair wrote to the CRU group.

Campbell writes, "In my experience, 'global warming' is already a bit of a public relations problem with the media."

To which Swedish Chief Climate Negotiator Bo Kjellen replied, "I agree with Nick that 'climate change' might be a better labelling than 'global warming'.

They chose the political option of moving the goalposts instead of the scientific option of revisiting their science. It is quite simple. If your predictions are wrong, your science is wrong.

Climate always changes, always has and always will. Gore and his minions know that there are enough people who either want to believe, don't understand, or don't care, that they can fool the world. As Elisabeth Noelle-Neumann explains,

> People with strong ethics are always at a disadvantage when debating people who have no ethics. This is because the public doesn't have the experience to know who is telling the truth, so they must base their opinion on other factors. We try to win arguments with truth, logic, and facts, but that requires more depth of understanding than most people possess. They tend to believe whichever party tells a story consistent with their own worldview. (Tell them what they want to hear . . . .) However, the non-scientific brain is most heavily influenced by figuring out "What does everyone else believe?" In areas of uncertainty people feel safe if they simply go along with the majority. This observation is based in part from Elisabeth Noelle-Neumann living and researching in Nazi Germany and her theory of the Spiral of Science. People fear isolation more than error, so they conform their beliefs to match what they perceive as the majority opinion. Or they simply remain silent. Our opponents rely on perceptions of majority opinion. The key is "perception" not reality. They only have to convince the public that a majority of "scientists" believes a certain way, even if that is untrue. If they are successful

creating this perception the others usually remain silent. However, when some don't remain silent, that explains why they MUST be marginalized to appear as fanatics and not credible. To some people, truth is not an objective fact, but only what you can convince a majority of the people to believe. That's because power resides with majority opinion, not with truth.[56]

The IPCC and political supporters have deceived people into believing that any climatic changes and natural weather events like hurricanes and floods are man-made. Global warming is therefore the grandest of all tyrannical schemes. They are trying to turn anthropogenic global warming into law like the law of gravity, when in fact the hypothesis that man's burning of fossil fuels is causing global warming is a hypothesis that has failed.

Most think the IPCC is the authority on global warming and climate change, when it is an agency set up to use climatology for a political agenda. Their role was to provide scientific proof that human production of CO_2 resulted in runaway global warming. They manipulated data and created false methods, while ignoring standard scientific procedures. They fooled most scientists, who simply accepted the claims at face value, not imagining there were scientists who would do such things. German meteorologist and physicist Klaus-Eckert Puls explains:

Ten years ago I simply parroted what the IPCC told us. One day I started checking the facts and data—first I started with a sense of doubt but then I became outraged when I discovered that much of what the IPCC and the media were telling us was sheer nonsense and was not even supported by

---

[56] http://www.afirstlook.com/docs/spiral.pdf

any scientific facts and measurements. To this day I still feel shame that as a scientist I made presentations of their science without first checking it.[57]

He added, "There's nothing we can do to stop it (climate change). Scientifically it is sheer absurdity to think we can get a nice climate by turning a CO2 adjustment knob."

Clearly Gore and the IPCC band of merry men are unaware of the history of science that determined centuries ago that science is never settled. As Sir Francis Bacon (1561–1626) wrote,

Another error is a conceit that the best has still prevailed and suppressed the rest: so as, if a man should begin the labor of a new search, he were but like to light upon somewhat formerly rejected, and by rejection brought into oblivion; as if the multitude, or the wisest for the multitude's sake, were not ready to give passage rather to that which is popular and superficial, than to that which is substantial and profound: for the truth is, that time seemeth to be of the nature of a river or stream, which carrieth down to us that which is light and blown up, and sinketh and drowneth that which is weighty and solid.

---

[57] http://notrickszone.com/2012/05/09/the-belief-that-co2-can-regulate-climate-is-sheer-absurdity-says-prominent-german-meteorologist/#sthash.4AtVilXE.TTbD8ydF.dpbs.

CHAPTER 6

CO2—DESIGNER POLLUTANT

For a number of reasons, carbon dioxide is one of the most important gases on earth and is necessary for the survival of all life on this planet. People need to ask why CO2, which is essential to plant life and by its production of oxygen to all life, became demonized as a pollutant that has to be drastically reduced. The IPCC claims it is at record levels when, at 396 ppmv, it is the lowest in 300 million years. If that level is reduced, plants do not grow as much and when the level reaches 150 ppmv, most plants are dead. To illustrate the contradictions in the urge to reduce levels, commercial greenhouses pump in extra CO2 to raise levels to 1200 ppmv that increase yield by a factor of four.

Two terms thrown around that few understand are "The Greenhouse Effect" and "Global Warming." They are linked for political effectiveness because people associate a greenhouse with high temperatures. In fact, the Earth's atmosphere doesn't work like a greenhouse. The objective of the UN agency the

Intergovernmental Panel on Climate Change (IPCC) was to isolate and demonize CO_2. It began when they were told to examine only human causes of global warming. There are three so-called greenhouse gases, water vapour is 95 percent by volume, CO_2 is 4 percent, and methane 0.36 percent. The IPCC immediately eliminated water vapour as they explained. "Water vapour is the most abundant and important greenhouse gas in the atmosphere. However, human activities have only a small direct influence on the amount of atmospheric water vapour." So the claim is human produced CO_2 is the effectively the cause of all temperature increase since 1950. The human portion of CO_2 in the atmosphere is 3.4 percent or 0.00272% of the total atmosphere. (Please see chart.)[58]

In the 2007 Report the IPCC wrote, "Water vapour is the most abundant and important greenhouse gas in the atmosphere. However, human activities have only a small direct influence on the amount of atmospheric water vapour."[59]

It is essentially impossible to determine the impact of 4 percent if you have very limited knowledge about 95 percent.

The IPCC tried to downplay the role of water vapor in affecting global temperatures by amplifying the role of CO_2 and CH_4. The range of numbers used to determine greenhouse effectiveness or Global Warming Potential (GWP) suggested people were just creating numbers—their formula was not scientific. The IPCC notes,

> The Global Warming Potential (GWP) is defined as the time-integrated RF (radio frequency) due to a pulse emission of a given component, relative to a pulse emission of an equal

mass of CO_2. The GWP was presented in the First IPCC Assessment (Houghton et al., 1990), stating "It must be stressed that there is no universally accepted methodology for combining all the relevant factors into a single global warming potential for greenhouse gas emissions." This is where the first deception begins. There are three gases that account for 99.9 percent of the GHG. They are water vapour (H_2O), carbon dioxide (CO_2), and methane (CH_4). The most important and most abundant by far, is water vapour at 95+ percent, while CO_2 is approximately 4 percent and methane less than 0.01 percent.

The question is who are the small group of elitists and how did the focus on CO_2 evolve from their objectives? They are members of the Club of Rome (COR) founded in 1968 and they promoted an agenda for global government. We need to show how CO_2 became pivotal to the scientific support and justification for their actions.

I mentioned Thomas Malthus and his book *An Essay on the Principle of Population* earlier. Now I need to explain how his work became the basis for establishing a socialist, one world, anti-Christian government.

Malthus was a political economist concerned about what he saw as the decline of living conditions in nineteenth century England. He blamed the decline on three elements: the overproduction of young, the inability of resources to keep up with the rising human population, and the irresponsibility of the lower classes. To combat this, Malthus suggested the family size of the lower class ought to be regulated such that poor families do not produce more children than they can support.

It wasn't the first time population and "carrying capacity" were linked, but this connection was different because it advocated government policy and control of population numbers. Charles Darwin was one of the strongest advocates of Malthus and took a copy of Malthus's book on his famous voyage. Malthus's theory would be instrumental in formulating Darwin's evolutionary theory. In his autobiography Darwin wrote,

> In October 1838, that is, fifteen months after I had begun my systematic inquiry, I happened to read for amusement Malthus on Population, and being well prepared to appreciate the struggle for existence which everywhere goes on from long-continued observation of the habits of animals and plants, it at once struck me that under these circumstances favourable variations would tend to be preserved, and unfavourable ones to be destroyed. The results of this would be the formation of a new species. Here, then I had at last got a theory by which to work.

The Club of Rome became Neo-Malthusians by taking Darwin's basic premise and expanding it to the claim that population would outgrow all resources. This identified two problems, limited resources and too many people. The Club brought focus on these with three books. One was Paul Ehrlich's *The Population Bomb* in 1968, which immediately became central to the environmental movement's focus that people were the problem.

The second book, *Limits to Growth,* appeared in 1972. It was a grossly simplistic study commissioned by the Club. It was the first to use computer models as scientific forecasters to justify public policy. They took current trends of resource use, and with a simple trend analysis, projected that forward against the then known estimates of the amount of resources. The third book was published in 1977, *Ecoscience Population, Resources, Environment.* It was co-authored by Holdren and Ehrlich and combined and concentrated the ideas of the first two books.

At that time, Holdren expressed truly frightening views about overpopulation. These included the following:

Women could be forced to abort their pregnancies, whether they wanted to or not.

The population at large could be sterilized by infertility drugs intentionally put into the nation's drinking water or in food.

Single mothers and teen mothers should have their babies seized from them against their will and given away to other couples to raise.

People who "contribute to social deterioration" (i.e., undesirables) "can be required by law to exercise reproductive responsibility"—in other words, be compelled to have abortions or be sterilized.

A transnational "Planetary Regime" should assume control of the global economy and also dictate the most intimate details of Americans' lives—using an armed international police force.

The question is how could such policies be implemented in the supposed liberties of democracy guaranteed in the United States? Holdren explained, in a format that emulates the technique used by all socialists regardless of the issue, create a false problem that justifies normally unacceptable actions as a resolution. "Indeed, it has been concluded that compulsory population-control laws, even including laws requiring compulsory abortion, could be sustained under the existing Constitution if the population crisis became sufficiently severe to endanger the society."[60]

The key to understanding what he is proposing is that he is the unseen person who has concluded that laws could be sustained. Then, he is the one who determines when the crisis is endangering society.

The Club of Rome (COR) then added a rider to the original Malthusian claim by arguing that all nations were growing in population and their exploitation of resources, but developed, industrialized nations were doing it at a much greater rate. It was necessary to slow them down. Maurice Strong, a member of the COR, expressed the idea obliquely to Elaine Dewar in her book *Cloak of Green* when he is quoted as saying,

> What if a small group of these world leaders were to conclude the principal risk to the earth comes from the actions of the rich countries? In order to save the planet, the group decides: Isn't the only hope for the planet that the industrialized civilizations collapse? Isn't it our responsibility to bring this about?[61]

How do you collapse the industrialized civilizations? They were built on fossil fuels, so if you cut off their supply, the engine of development would stall. Politically, that was an impossible objective, but you can also stop an engine by

---

[60] Andrew Curtis, *1984 Redux: Say Hello to "Big Brother,"* (Bloomington, IN: Author House, 20110), 281.
[61] http://mediamatters.org/blog/2010/05/13/beck-pushes-scary-conspiracy-theories-about-cli/164655.

blocking the exhaust. If you could show that the by-product of those industrialized engines, CO2, was causing runaway global warming, you could achieve the goal. Dewar then challenged Strong to explain how he would do this as a politician.

Strong said he was going to do it through the UN because, "He could raise his own money from whomever he liked, appoint anyone he wanted, and control the agenda."[62]

As Dewar explained after spending several days with Strong at the UN, "Strong was using the UN as a platform to sell a global environment crisis and the Global Governance Agenda."

So CO2 became the demon gas that was causing population increase and development, both threatening the future of the planet. Strong set up a two-pronged system to control the agenda. The first was the political side that culminated in Agenda 21; the second was the United Nations Framework Convention of Climate Change (UNFCCC) that gave the very narrow definition of climate change as only those caused by humans to the Intergovernmental Panel on Climate Change (IPCC). All this came together at the Rio 1992 conference that Strong organized as chair of the United Nations Environment Program (UNEP), a division he created. Part of the Declaration from that conference says,

> There is also general agreement that unsustainable consumption and production patterns are contributing to the unsustainable use of natural resources and environmental degradation as well as to the reinforcement of social inequities and of poverty with the above-mentioned consequences for demographic parameters.

---

[62] Elaine Dewar, Cloak of Green: The Links between Key Environmental Groups, Government and Big Business, (Torinto, ON; Lorimer, 1995).

So CO2 became the focus of their anti-Christian socialist agenda, which believes people are an aberration, not children of God. This anti-humanity theme underlies environmentalism and is expressed in various comments.

In a 1990 Greenpeace Report on Global Warming. The author notes, "Carbon dioxide is added to the atmosphere, naturally and unnaturally." The unnatural refers to the human contribution, so if what we do is unnatural then, by default, we are unnatural. German philosopher Goethe dealt with this inanity when he said, "The unnatural—that too is natural."

David Graber, a research biologist with the US National Park Service, said,

> Human happiness, and certainly human fecundity, are not as important as a wild and healthy planet. I know social scientists who remind me that people are part of nature, but it isn't true. Somewhere along the line—at about a billion years ago—we quit the contract and became a cancer. We have become a plague upon ourselves and upon the earth. It is cosmically unlikely that the developed world will choose to end its orgy of fossil energy consumption, and the Third World its suicidal consumption of landscape. Until such time as Homo Sapiens should decide to rejoin nature, some of us can only hope for the right virus to come along.

Likely this is where Prince Philip, grand central figure to the Illuminati, got his idea.

In 1988, Britain's Prince Philip expressed the wish that, should he be reincarnated, he would want to be a deadly virus that would reduce world population.

Ingrid Newkirk of People for the Ethical Treatment of Animals (PETA) said,

> Mankind is a cancer; we're the biggest blight on the face of the earth. If you haven't given voluntary human extinction much thought before, the idea of a world with no people in it may seem strange. But if you give it a chance, I think you might agree that the extinction of Homo Sapiens would mean survival for millions if not billions, of earth-dwelling species. Phasing out the human race will solve every problem on earth, social and environmental.[63]

Writing in *Audubon*, Richard Connif, an American non-fiction writer specializing in human and animal behavior, wrote, "Among environmentalists sharing two or three beers, the notion is quite common that if only some calamity could wipe out the entire human race, other species might once again have a chance." Think of the insanity of the depopulation proponents who want to wipe out a majority of the population, and yet they too have families. It reeks of the idea that they feel they and their families are exempt from this culling. It begs the question—who gets to decide who lives and who dies? But then who can get in the mind of a megalomaniac to figure out their bizarre twisted thoughts?

Consider the Canadian environmentalist David Suzuki and his bizarre comments in a 1992 keynote address to the Environmental Grantmakers Association, "Economics is a very species-chauvinistic idea. No other species on earth—and there are may be 30 million of them—has had the nerve to put forth a concept called economics, in which one species, us, declares

---

[63] *Reader's Digest*, June, 1990.

the right to put value on everything else on earth, in the living and nonliving world."

He is incorrect. All other species assign one value to everything else. It is food or it is not food. Humans put a very wide range of values on everything; indeed, the differences between humans and all other animals is so great that Darwin's contemporary, Alfred Russell Wallace, said these differences alone invalidate Darwin's evolutionary theory. Suzuki also has the number of species wrong. Thirty million is a gross underestimate. A study by PLoS Biology says, ". . . A staggering 86 percent of all species on land and 91 percent of those in the seas have yet to be discovered, described, and catalogued."[64]

Of course no other species has the ability to develop concepts like economics. Lack of accurate data and misinterpretation of mechanisms allow the misapplication of the role and function of CO_2. While adding carbon dioxide to the atmosphere causes far less warming than previously feared, it has a positive effect on plant life. With more carbon dioxide in the air, plants grow better in warmer and cooler temperatures and wetter and drier soils, make better use of soil nutrients, and resist diseases and pests better, increasing their fruit production, expanding their range, and greening the earth. This makes more food available to all other creatures, especially—as agricultural yields rise—making food more affordable for the world's poor. This is ironically the exact opposite of the views expressed by the people we have introduced you to in this book. Green energy projects, such as substituting wind, solar, and other low-density energy sources for coal, oil, and natural gas therefore hurt the poor not only by raising energy (and all other) prices but also by reducing

---

[64] http://www.sciencedaily.com/releases/2011/08/110823180459.htm.

food production. These energy projects also hurt the rest of life on earth by depriving it of the fertilizing effect of heightened carbon dioxide.

Truly, "The heavens declare the glory of God; and the firmament proclaims his handiwork" (Ps. 19:1). Carbon dioxide, on which life depends, beautifully reveals the Creator's wisdom and care for all of His creation—people, animals, plants, and the earth itself. The fact that God's own handiwork is demonized as harmful instead of deemed essential to life, illustrates the corruption of science to push an anti-human, anti-Christian agenda. But for what purpose, you ask? Why? Simply put, the anti-Christian Technocracy wants a New World Order. Chapter 1 discussed the history and evolution of this objective. It has generally failed through political systems such as National Socialism in Germany and communism in the Soviet Union and elsewhere. Environmentalism and global warming provided the next vehicle for achieving the objective.

CHAPTER 7

New World Order Disorder

"No one will enter the New World Order unless he or she will make a pledge to worship Lucifer. No one will enter the New Age unless he will take a Luciferian Initiation."

—David Spangler
Director of Planetary Initiative, United Nations

In a speech at the Waldorf-Astoria Hotel in New York on April 27, 1961, John F. Kennedy said,

The very word *secrecy* is repugnant in a free and open society, and we are as a people inherently and historically opposed to secret societies, to secret oaths, and to secret proceedings. We decided long ago that the dangers of excessive and unwarranted concealment of pertinent facts far outweighed the dangers that are cited to justify it. Even today, there is little value in opposing the threat of a closed society by imitating its arbitrary restrictions. Even today, there is little value in insuring the survival of our nation if our traditions do not survive with it. And there is very grave danger that an announced need for increased security will be seized upon by those anxious to expand its meaning to the very limits of official censorship and concealment.

That I do not intend to permit to the extent that it is in my control. And no official of my Administration, whether his rank is high or low, civilian or military, should interpret my words here tonight as an excuse to censor the news, to stifle dissent, to cover up our mistakes or to withhold from the press and the public the facts they deserve to know . . . . I can only say that the danger has never been clearer and its presence has never been more imminent. It requires a change in outlook, a change in tactics, and a change in missions—by the government, by the people, by every businessman or labor leader, and by every newspaper. For we are opposed around the world by a monolithic and ruthless conspiracy that relies primarily on covert means for expanding its sphere of influence—on infiltration instead of invasion, on subversion instead of elections, on intimidation instead of free choice, on guerrillas by night instead of armies by day. It is a system which has conscripted vast human and material resources into the building of a tightly knit, highly efficient machine that combines military, diplomatic, intelligence, economic, scientific and political operations. Its preparations are concealed, not published. Its mistakes are buried, not headlined. Its dissenters are silenced, not praised. No expenditure is questioned, no rumor is printed, no secret is revealed.

Today, there is no doubt he was speaking about the Fabian Socialists (British socialists whose purpose is to advance the Imperial and the Communist principles) and their efforts to enslave and depopulate the planet as well as dominate through complete totalitarianism.

The Fabian Socialists, aka the Marxist cabal, call this their New World Order, starting with Mayer Amschel Rothschild of Frankfurt. He asked the "apostate" Jesuit Adam Weishaupt to design an organization with which Mayer could rule the world by means of money. On May 1, 1776, this secret order for the New World had been presented to Rothschild. Weishaupt called the order the Illuminati, which after the Wilhelmsbad Freemason conference in 1781, infiltrated freemasonry and still survives. Upon his return home from the conference, Comte de Virieu, a Mason, said: "I can only tell you that all this is very much more serious than you think. The conspiracy which is being woven is so well thought out, that it will be impossible for the Monarchy and the Church to escape it."

This Illuminati movement—today called illuminism by the European Union—is the belief of the Illuminati in their specialized and proprietary claim of special enlightenment. It has its roots in the "master race" concept of the Pharisaic Talmud, as Mayer Rothschild was a "pious" Talmud Jew and proponent of creating a master race.

Brothers Aldous and Julian Huxley, as well as Bertrand Russell, introduced the idea of global scientific dictatorship by means of eugenics and by making mankind slaves through mass psychology. But more than that, they want to make people love their slavery. Once completely established, their dictatorship will be impossible to abolish. These agendas were funded by Rockefeller Foundations, Ford, Carnegie, Mellon, Harriman, and Morgan, taking shape at the turn of the 20th century, with Hitler further developing the ideas and the system in the Holocaust. After World War II, eugenics had to split up into population control, genetics, environmentalism, and mental hygiene. The eugenicists are using tools like genetic manipulation and technology to further their insidious agenda. Their aim is global mind control over a reduced humanity consisting of upgraded individuals. Servitude, inequality, and extinction of the weak are part of the playbook. Award-winning author and researcher Edwin Black wrote an authoritative history of eugenics in his book, *War Against the Weak*, in which he explained that, "the incremental effort to transform eugenics into human genetics forged an entire worldwide infrastructure," with the founding of the Institute for Human Genetics in Copenhagen in 1938, led by a Rockefeller Foundation eugenicist. It was financed with money from the Rockefeller Foundation. While not abandoning the eugenics goals, the re-branded eugenics movement "claimed to be eradicating poverty and saving the environment."

Aldous Huxley in 1932 wrote *Brave New World*, in which he looked at the emergence of the scientific dictatorships of the future. In his 1958 essay, "Brave New World Revisited," Huxley examined how far the world had come in the short period since his first book and where the world was heading. Huxley wrote, "In economics, the equivalent of a beautifully composed work of art is the smoothly running factory in which the workers are perfectly adjusted to the machines." Huxley further explained that "The twenty-first century, I suppose, will be the era of World Controllers, the scientific caste system and Brave New World."

In a 1962 speech at UC Berkeley, Huxley spoke primarily of the "Ultimate Revolution" that focuses on "behavioral controls" of people:

> If you are going to control any population for any length of time, you must bring in an element of getting people to

consent to what is happening to them. We are in process of developing a whole series of techniques, which will enable the controlling oligarchy—who have always existed and will presumably always exist—to get people to love their servitude. I think there are going to be scientific dictatorships in many parts of the world. If you can get people to consent to the state of servitude—then you are likely to have a much more stable, a much more lasting society; much more easily controllable society than you would if you were relying wholly on clubs, and firing squads and concentration camps.

In 1952, Bertrand Russell wrote the book, *The Impact of Science on Society*, that explained,

I think the subject which will be of most importance politically is mass psychology. Its importance has been enormously increased by the growth of modern methods of propaganda. Of these the most influential is what is called "education." Religion plays a part, though a diminishing one; the Press, the cinema and the radio. What is essential in mass psychology is the art of persuasion. I see no reason why a "scientific dictatorship" should be unstable. After all, most civilized and semi-civilized countries known to history have had a large class play an increasing part. Slaves or serfs completely subordinate to their owners. When the government controls the distribution of food, its power is absolute so long as it can count on the police and the armed forces. And their loyalty can be secured by giving them some of the privileges of the governing class. I do not see how any internal movement of revolt can ever bring freedom to the oppressed in a modern scientific dictatorship.[65]

---

[65] Bertrand Russell, *The Impact of Science on Society*, (New York, NY: Routledge, 1985), 66.

As you can now see, the green movement, including the global warming fraud, has never been about the climate but was always about setting up a one-world government. Leaders of the British eugenics-cum-environmental movement, led by Prince Philip, first hatched the lie of human-induced climate change more than three decades ago. Margaret Thatcher's science guru Sir Crispin Tickell, along with eugenicist Sir Frank MacFarlane Burnet, first championed it. It has nothing to do with science or saving the planet. It is an imperial Fabian Society doctrine to justify eliminating billions of human beings in order to secure the continued world rule by the still existing British Empire, the core of whose power is the now-collapsing, privately controlled international monetary system. Prince Philip and his friends keep pushing the global warming fraud, targeting human CO_2 emissions as its ostensible cause, because CO_2 is the natural, and necessary, by-product of the industrial activity that sustains human life. Human life is not a priority for these megalomaniacs. The end to them justifies the means, even if it means wiping out 6 billion people.

In 1970, Zbigniew Brzezinski wrote about "the gradual appearance of a more controlled and directed society…. Such a society would be dominated by an elite whose claim to political power would rest on allegedly superior scientific know-how. Unhindered by the restraints of traditional liberal values, this elite would not hesitate to achieve its political ends by using the latest modern techniques for influencing public behavior and keeping society under close surveillance and control."[66]

It just so happens that elites who propagate this ideology also happen to view the masses as intellectually inferior; thus, there can be no social equality, individual freedom, or liberty.

---

[66] Zbigniew Brzezinski, Between Two Ages: *America's Role in the Technetronic Era*, (Westport, CN: Praeger 1982).

Eugenics is about the social organization and control of humanity. Ultimately, eugenics is about the engineering of inequality. In genetics, elites found a way to take discrimination down to the DNA.

In a 2001 issue of *Science* magazine, Garland Allen, a scientific historian, wrote about genetics as a modern form of eugenics. Victorian progressive Francis Galton, geographer, statistician, and first cousin of Charles Darwin, coined the term *eugenics* in 1883. It meant to him "truly- or well-born" and referred to a plan to encourage the "best people" in society to have more children (positive eugenics) and to discourage or prevent the "worst elements" of society from having many, if any, children (negative eugenics). It fit Malthusian ideas well. For the wealthy benefactors who supported eugenics, such as the Carnegie, Rockefeller, Harriman, and Kellogg philanthropies, it provided a means of social control in a period of unprecedented upheaval and violence. John D. Rockefeller III founded the Population Council in 1952, funded by the Rockefeller Brothers Fund. It is rooted in the eugenics movement and works for "reproductive health," which means contraception. But the Rockefeller family has a long history of support for eugenics—funding Hitler's Chief Eugenicist Ernst Rüdin extensively. Thus in 1934, a Rockefeller "progress report" (by one of the division heads) asks,

> Can we develop so sound and extensive a genetics that we can hope to breed, in the future, superior men? Free humanity faces the most monumental decision we have ever been presented with: do we feed and fuel the global political awakening into a true human psycho-social revolution of the mind, creating a new global political economy which empowers and liberates

all of humanity; or . . . do we fall silently into a "brave new world" of a global scientific oppression, the likes of which have never before been experienced, and whose dominance would never be more difficult to challenge and overcome. We are not powerless before this great ideational beast. We have, at our very fingertips, the ability to use technology to re-shape the world so that it benefits the peoples and not simply the powerful.[67]

The New World Order's tentacles reach across the oceans to America, Europe, and the rest of the world with strong connections to the European Royal Families, the Rothschilds, the Pilgrims Society, the Royal Institute of International Affairs (Chatham House), the Bank of England, selected banking and financial institutions, Friends of Israel Groups and so many other elite groups, including the Illuminati-controlled Freemans. These evil Luciferians control their counterparts, including the Rockefellers, the Council of Foreign Relations, the Trilateral Commission, the Bilderberg Group, and the Federal Reserve Bank, among others.

Consider what unashamed predatory Globalist David Rockefeller said in his book, "Some even believe we (the Rockefeller family) are part of a secret cabal working against the best interests of the United States, characterizing my family and me as 'internationalists' and of conspiring with others around the world to build a more integrated global political and economic structure—one world, if you will. If that's the charge, I stand guilty, and I am proud of it."[68]

---

[67] http://www.crossroad.to/Quotes/brainwashing/rockefeller-mind-control.htm.
[68] David Rockefeller, *Memoirs,* (Random House, 2002), 405.

These groups control the UN and all its respective departments, the WHO (World Health Organization), the ICJ (International Court of Justice), and the entire judicial system, the educational system, the foundation of the banking and financial system, the mainstream media and, believe it or not, NATO, The North Atlantic Treaty Organization also called the North Atlantic Alliance, which is its military arm, and even the spread of Islam.[69] One can clearly see that the Cold War as such has never ended and the Crusades continue. It is clear in the "false flags," that is, covert operations designed to deceive in such a way that the operations appear as though they are being carried out by entities, groups, or nations other than those who actually planned and executed them.

The aim is to impose not just tyranny, but to dictate what you can and cannot do. In other words complete subjugation. Soon it will be impossible for you to go to the bank, go shopping, go to the hospital, or see a doctor. In addition to this, the powers that be want to implement a cashless society and they are shockingly close to achieving it. Consider in London, buses will start in July accepting cards only—no more cash. Currency Exchanges are now offering cards instead of cash that they market as being safer in travel. In Manchester, all the shops on Chorlton Street will no longer accept cash—only cards. This is a test to see if society is ready for the change.

On May 14, 2015, an article at Zero Hedge Financial explains how the globalist bankers were pushing for a cashless society.[70] The loss of privacy with Big Brother and the electronic bondage is evident. The powers that be are tracking, hacking, and attacking everyone in society, preparing our generation for

---

[69] Paul McGuire, Mass Awakening, (Hoboken, NJ: M House Publishers, 2015).

[70] http://www.zerohedge.com/news/2015-05-04/why-powers-be-are-pushing-cashless-society

the Mark of the Beast. Revelation 13:16–17: "And he causeth all, both small and great, rich and poor, free and bond, to receive a mark in their right hand, or in their foreheads, And that no man might buy or sell, save he that had the mark, or the name of the beast, or the number of his name.[71]

As I said about Marx earlier, the elite feel that they are entrusted—due to their supposed "innate" superior intelligence and specialization—to control society and reshape it as they see fit, to actively mold and construct public opinion and ideas. They believe that people are essentially irrational, emotional beings and must be controlled by an elite, or else the world would be in chaos. This is what underpins the ideas of "stability" and "order." The Technological Revolution, especially the Internet, has fostered an Information Revolution that has fed a global political awakening. Simultaneously, the Technological Revolution has led to free humanity being faced with the dominating threat of a truly global elite, who have at their hands the technology to impose a truly global system of control: a global scientific dictatorship with an increasing ability to control the very biology and psychology of the individual. They want complete enslavement of people whom they see as cannon fodder. What I've just described is serfdom by stealth through complete subjugation and global enslavement. This is *Brave New World* meets *1984*, and it's not coming—it's here.

"Do we achieve world order through chaos or insight?"
—Henry Kissinger

---

[71] Revelation 13:16–17 King James Version (KJV).

CHAPTER 8

AGENDA 21: THE UN PLAN FOR GLOBAL ENSLAVEMENT

"Isn't the only hope for this planet that the industrialized civilization collapse? Isn't it our responsibility to bring that about?"

—Maurice Strong
1992 UN Summit in Rio de Janeiro

A braham Lincoln is credited with numerous statements that may or may not have originated with him. One of these statements reveals a profound human and political truth. He held that in general people have two reasons why they justify every decision they make. The first is a public reason, and it appears logical. The second reason is hidden and based on emotion. The second is the real motivation for the decision. Unless we fully grasp a person's second or "hidden" reason, we will never fully understand the real motives behind the actions. Nefarious crusaders behind the green agenda, including the anthropogenic global warming (AGW) movement, are not primarily motivated to address future global temperatures and subsequent results. Rather, they want a New World Order that requires destruction of capitalist, free enterprise economies, and elimination of privately owned land where people acquiesce to their global Socialist Marxist regime of totalitarianism. How will they implement their hellish regime? The answer is in implementation of a doctrine for the twenty-first century presented to the 1992 Rio conference entitled Agenda 21.

The term *Sustainable Development* was first introduced to the world in a 1987 report (Our Common Future) produced by the United Nations World Commission on Environmental and Development, authored by Gro Harlem Brundtland, VP of the World Socialist Party.[72] The term was first offered as official UN policy in 1992, in a document called UN Sustainable Development Agenda 21, issued at the UN's Earth Summit, today referred to simply as Agenda 21. Agenda 21 is the brainchild of a Marxist New Age and Rothschild/Rockefeller minion, a colleague of Mikhail Gorbachev and strongly suspected thief, Maurice Strong, as we mentioned earlier. It is not surprising that Agenda 21 mainly uses the CO2 lie as a pretext. This lie stems from the ideas of Edmund de Rothschild, and in Rio, Maurice Strong inoculated it into the ignorant world of elected politicians indelibly, despite all the illogic. The best definition of Agenda 21 comes right from the UN itself. In 1993, the UN published "Agenda 21: The Earth Summit Strategy to Save Our Planet."[73]

Agenda 21 proposes an array of actions intended for implementation by every person on earth that call "for specific

---

[72] http://www.un-documents.net/our-common-future.pdf.
[73] Daniel Sitarz, *Agenda 21: The Earth Summit Strategy to Save Our Planet,* (Hauppauge, NY: Nova Publishing, 1993).

changes in the activities of all people." Effective execution of Agenda 21 will require a profound reorientation of all humans, unlike anything the world has ever experienced.

According to its authors, the objective of sustainable development is to integrate economic, social, and environmental policies in order to achieve reduced consumption, social equity, and the preservation and restoration of biodiversity. Believers in sustainability insist that every societal decision be based on environmental impact, focusing on three components: global land use, global education, and global population control and reduction.

SOCIAL EQUITY (SOCIAL JUSTICE)

They describe social justice as the right and opportunity of all people "to benefit equally from the resources afforded us by society and the environment" achieved through redistribution of wealth. Private property is a social injustice since not everyone can build wealth from it. National sovereignty is a social injustice. All are part of Agenda 21 policy.

ECONOMIC PROSPERITY

Public Private Partnerships (PPP) refers to special dealings between government and certain chosen corporations that get tax breaks, grants, and the government's power of eminent domain to implement sustainable policy. Government-sanctioned monopolies.

Local Sustainable Development policies include smart growth, wild land projects, resilient cities, regional visioning projects, STAR sustainable communities, green jobs, green building codes, "going green," alternative energy, local visioning, facilitators, regional planning, historic preservation, conservation easements, development rights, sustainable farming, comprehensive planning, growth management, and consensus. J. Gary Lawrence, advisor to President Clinton's Council on Sustainable Development, said,

> Participating in a UN advocated planning process would very likely bring out many of the conspiracy-fixated groups and individuals in our society . . . This segment of our society who fear "one-world government" and a UN invasion of the United States through which our individual freedom would be stripped away would actively work to defeat any elected official who joined "the conspiracy" by undertaking Agenda 21. So we call our process something else, such as comprehensive planning, growth management or smart growth.[74]

In Rio in 1992, heads of state and governments from 181 countries adopted this action program for the twenty-first century: Agenda 21 that is designed "to remove imminent threats, limit excessive consumption of resources and jointly try to steer development in a more sustainable direction. It calls on people worldwide to collaborate on local action plans and initiatives for sustainable development."

AGENDA 21 AND PRIVATE PROPERTY

"Land . . . cannot be treated as an ordinary asset, controlled by individuals and subject to the pressures and inefficiencies of the market. Private land ownership is also a principal instrument of

---

[74] http://americanpolicy.org/agenda21/.

accumulation and concentration of wealth, therefore contributes to social injustice." This is taken from the 1976 UN's Habitat I Conference Report.

"Private land use decisions are often driven by strong economic incentives that result in several ecological and aesthetic consequences . . . The key to overcoming it is through public policy. . . ." Report from the President's Council on Sustainable Development, page 112.[75]

"Current lifestyles and consumption patterns of the affluent middle class—involving high meat intake, use of fossil fuels, appliances, home and work air conditioning, and suburban housing are not sustainable." Maurice Strong, Secretary General of the UN's Earth Summit, 1992. This is summarized in the Local Agenda 21 Guide: Everything is to be standardized; all individuality destroyed; our hard-earned prosperity to be globally redistributed by need; (1.0) the "right persons" be undemocratically installed (cf. 2.2.6); obedience to be rewarded and dissidence to be punished (6.4); reporting (6.1) to take place, and a systemic/global perspective (4.0) to be intertwined into any local decision—the elements of the Rothschild/Rockefeller world state standardized locally for the great screwdriver; basic elements are consensus and sustainability (1.3.2), which excludes differences of opinion. The Germans know that this is the nature of dictatorship—whether Nazi or Communist. It is the enforcement of the Order of the Illuminati program for world government, founded by Johann Adam Weishaupt.

Simply put, Agenda 21 derived from the Earth Summit in Rio in 1992, and as I stated, the person behind it was the Summit's Secretary General, UNEP Chairman Maurice Strong.

---

[75] http://clinton2.nara.gov/PCSD/lettrep.html.

As mentioned previously, Strong hijacked gullible world leaders on behalf of his friend Edmund de Rothschild, had CO2 criminalized, and introduced the Global Environmental Facility, a Rothschild bank. It has governmental representatives from 179 countries on its board to ensure that we pay Rothschild for grabbing up to 30 percent of the land of the world as forfeited collateral—"wildernesses." Agenda 21 removes private landownership just like the Highland Clearances of the eighteenth century. In this case, the people are herded into urbanized areas in order to facilitate monitoring us and indoctrinating our children to the corporate New World Order Earth Charter initiative's rule of the earth and its Luciferian ideology.

Strong is not just the brain behind Agenda 21 but is also the connection between the Club of Rome and the UN Agenda 21 push for a collectivist global government. He is now living in Beijing, where he is informally in touch with the Communist UN Secretary-General Ban Ki-moon. Apparently, the reason for Strong's exile in China is a scandal in the UN's corrupt Oil-for-Food relief program for Iraq, where Mr. Strong issued a UN cheque for $988,885—which sum was secretly delivered to—Mr. Strong.[76] Over many years, Mr. Strong shaped the UN agenda in which public conferences became largely a façade for decisions already brokered behind the scenes by him. He is an adviser to the Communist Chinese government and is also believed to have sanctuary in China because of his cousin, Anne Louise Strong, a Marxist who lived with Mao Tse Tung (the greatest mass murderer in history) for two years before she died in 1970.

---

[76] Micha-el Thomas Hays, *Rise of the New World Order: The Culling of Man,* (Washington DC: Samaritan Sentinel, 2013), 283.

From 1971, Maurice Strong served as a trustee for the Rockefeller Foundation and the Aspen Institute. Later, he also served as an advisor to the Rockefeller Foundation and was a member of the Club of Rome. He was a co-founder of the Canada-China Business Council in 1978. He had the generous support of Laurence Rockefeller. Maurice Strong was introduced to Edmund de Rothschild at the World Wilderness Conference in September 1987. At that conference he said,

> One of the most important initiatives that is open here for your consideration is that of the Conservation Banking Program. As mentioned this morning, we have here the person who really is the source of this very significant concept. Many of the energy developments that we have seen have come from his early anticipation of our energy needs, Edmund de Rothschild.

Edmund then gave a speech about Global Warming and shipping CO_2 to the poles. David Rockefeller swore conference attendees to secrecy.

Strong co-founded the Earth Council Institute in 1992 and has been its chairman ever since. Mikhail Gorbachev (president of the USSR until 1991) helped in its creation. In 1994, Maurice Strong, Mikhail Gorbachev, and Ruud Lubbers joined again to launch a civil society, the Earth Charter Initiative, the mission of which is, "To establish a sound ethical foundation for the emerging global society and to help build a sustainable world based on respect for nature, universal human rights, economic justice, and a culture of peace."

Since 1992, more than 1,300 local authorities from 31 countries have responded to the Agenda 21 mandate by developing their Local Agenda 21 action plans for sustainable development. The task of mobilizing and technically supporting Local Agenda 21 planning in these communities has been led by the International Council for Local Global Summit Environmental Initiatives (ICLEI) and national associations of local government. The framework presented in the Agenda 21 Planning Guide was derived from real-life Local Agenda 21 planning efforts around the world. It is available to local governments as a blueprint for implementing Agenda 21 in their region. In the publication titled, "The Local Agenda 21 Planning Guide" (LA21PG), the transition to sustainable development is not a soft option, but an imperative for our survival and well-being. The guide says that it is going to require a great deal of courage and commitment from all sectors, including municipalities, to ensure its success.[77]

The LA21PG goes on to say, "Even as urban areas increasingly represent a concentration of our greatest social, economic, and environmental problems, they offer opportunities for some of the most effective solutions. The real world actions and decisions will determine whether the vision of Rio will be fulfilled and the agreements reached there implemented."

In 1996, Strong said, of the many programs that have resulted from the Earth Summit, none is more promising or important than this one.

Communism is a tool of the corporate capitalists who own the world. They want to abolish the middle class, so that they only have to control the proletariat, the "useless eaters," whose number they are trying to reduce by all means. At least the Chinese were open in their enforceable one-child policy.

---

[77] http://www.postsustainabilityinstitute.org/uploads/4/4/6/6/4466371/iclei.la21flyer.pdf.

Agenda 21 is not just about climate; it is simply the vehicle to say the sky is falling, that humans are the cause, and we will save you if you admit to your sins. It is precise planning of every aspect of your life according to communist principles, as you discover when you read the Local Agenda 21 Planning Guide that entails full spectrum dominance on every human being. Agenda 21 was created by the UN, but it was really masterminded by the global elite. It involves the World Bank, the ICLEI (International Council for Local Environmental Initiatives), and Local Governments for Sustainability, which is an international association of local governments and national and regional local government organizations that have made a commitment to sustainable development. More than 1,000 cities, towns, counties, and their associations in sixty-eight countries comprise ICLEI's growing membership. ICLEI continues to play an active role in promoting and facilitating the implementation of Local Agenda 21. It also reports on local progress and performance at the global level through the United Nations and other international forums, rewarding progress and punishing negligence. It redistributes our wealth, so it is bound to produce poverty as it did in the Soviet Union, since it just rewards sustainability; ordinary jobs are killed for every unproductive green job created. It is a result already experienced in countries like Spain where two jobs were lost for every green job created. It does not reward work—thus it is sure to diminish productivity drastically, creating a lack of commodities like food and energy—all witnessed in the Soviet Union.

Despite disclosure of the leaked Climatic Research Unit (CRU) e-mails and the failure of the Copenhagen climate summit in 2009, the United Nations is pushing ahead for a global carbon tax that will bankroll the expansion of world government as globalists attempt to make Americans pay for the evisceration of their sovereignty and future prosperity. The next effort to achieve their goal occurs in Paris in September 2015. The sinister anthropogenic global warming (AGW) scheme includes national government leaders, prominent politicians, members of the mainstream media conglomerates, and private organizations.

Working in lockstep with Agenda 21, the Obama camp is now working to forge a sweeping international climate change agreement to compel nations to cut their planet-warming fossil fuel emissions, but without ratification from Congress. Negotiators are meeting with diplomats to broker a deal to reduce their carbon pollution. Obama's climate negotiators are devising a politically binding deal that would basically name and shame countries into cutting their emissions. Obama operates in a cloistered environment but when the radical red greenies come calling and demand action, he moves. He will enact the Saul Alinsky playbook, which means shutting down the coal mines, steel mills, commercial fisheries, oil rigs, industry and assembly lines, and public utilities, violating the law and the Constitution. Even if Congress won't rubber stamp it then, of course, he will impose it like a dictator. He uses the Environmental Protection Agency (EPA) to introduce rules and regulations to fulfill candidate Obama's pledge to bankrupt the coal industry and enact a de facto cap and trade regime the president couldn't get through Congress. The man who said his nomination marked the moment the seas began to recede and the planet began to cool and heal now plans to deal the rule of law and the US Constitution yet another blow. It involves a Kyoto-like "accord" that he can use as moral cover for further destroying the US.

economy, in lieu of an actual climate change "treaty" that must be ratified by two-thirds of a Senate that has already unanimously rejected such a pact.

I explained earlier how John Holdren, when discussing forced abortions, showed how they would use the Constitution. It is the perversity of their thinking that the very document designed to protect freedom of choice and basic individual rights would be used to force their sacrifice for what they determine to be the common good. It would then be aligned with the tenets of the UN Agenda 21, which extends it to the global common good. Under the veil of warm and fuzzy feel-good but meaningless slogans, terms like *eco-friendly* and *sustainable development* and *social equity*, a self-described "new world order" is being systematically implemented. It is organized around the principle that nature is the most fundamental truth and requires all spheres of society to conform to that principle, under the government of ruling elite.

At the 1992 Earth Summit, Maurice Strong also introduced a new socialist concept he called social justice that soon morphed into environmental justice.

In an interview explaining his fundamental belief in global government, Maurice Strong said the "right of all the people to benefit equally from resources afforded by society and the environment would be accomplished by the socialist Communist redistribution of wealth." When asked to explain in more detail what his concept of environmental justice might look like in practical terms, Strong told a reporter, "Licenses to have babies incidentally is something that I got in trouble for some years ago suggesting even in Canada that this might be necessary at some point at least some restrictions on the right to have children."

Doesn't this sound eerily similar to the writings of Karl Marx in 1875, "from each according to his abilities to each according to his needs." America's first black president would later say, "We have to spread the wealth around a little."

Like the Wizard of Oz who hid behind his curtain, pulled levers and made threatening noises that frighten the Cowardly Lion, the Tin Man, Dorothy, and everybody in Oz, a small group of globalist wizards hiding behind a "green curtain" created one imagined environmental disaster after another. For decades, the wizard scared everyone with scientific eco-babble and demands for obedience to their agenda for the twenty-first century.

In reality, the green tsunami of globalism operates completely in the open and they have set their global agenda and it's coming soon to a local community near you calling for dramatically increasing urbanization and forcing populations out of rural areas and into densely populated massive megacities complete with stack-and-pack micro apartments controlled by technocrats with the ability to control every aspect of one's life. When completed, it would be what I call complete hell on earth.

As Aldous Huxley put it: "We will make them love their serfdom."

CHAPTER 9

CONNECTING THE GREEN DOTS: DEPOPULATION

Death and the management of who lives and who dies has become the central organizing principle of the twenty-first century. It was a principle of World Wars I and II, along with the despotic regimes of Mao, Pol Pot, Stalin, Lenin, Hitler, and others who took hundreds of millions of lives, and of the folks we have introduced you to in this book. World population is completely out of control according to many of the people we have talked about. Let us consider some of the many ways to cause the death of large numbers of people, and many were listed by Malthus as natural controls of population. These include war, pestilence, disease, and starvation. Other methods used include the build-up and use of nuclear, chemical, and biological agents, weapons, and warfare; the poisoning and contamination of the planet's food and water supplies; the introduction and use of deadly pharmaceutical drugs in society; weather modification and geo-engineering, the promotion of homosexuality to limit population growth; forced sterilization, forced vaccinations, abortion, and euthanasia.

Eugenics was the racist pseudoscience determined to wipe away all human beings deemed "unfit," preserving only those who conformed to a Nordic stereotype. But the concept of a white, blond-haired, blue-eyed master Nordic race didn't originate with Hitler. The idea was created in the United States and cultivated in California, decades before Hitler came to power. California eugenicists played an important, although little known, role in the American eugenics movement's campaign for ethnic cleansing. Elements of the philosophy were enshrined as national policy by forced sterilization and segregation laws, as well as marriage restrictions enacted in twenty-seven states. In 1909, California became the third state to adopt such laws. Ultimately, eugenics practitioners coercively sterilized some 60,000 Americans, barred the marriage of thousands, forcibly segregated thousands in "colonies," and persecuted untold numbers in ways we are just learning. Before World War II, nearly half of coercive sterilizations were done in California, and even after the war, the state accounted for a third of all such surgeries.

Hitler and his henchmen victimized an entire continent and exterminated millions in his quest for a co-called "master race."

Much of the spiritual guidance and political agitation for the American eugenics movement came from California's quasi-autonomous eugenic societies, such as the Pasadena-based Human Betterment Foundation and the California branch of the American Eugenics Society, which coordinated much of their activity with the Eugenics Research Society in Long Island, New York. These organizations, which functioned as part of a closely-knit network, published racist eugenic newsletters and pseudoscientific journals, such as *Eugenical News* and *Eugenics*, and propagandized for the Nazis.

Eugenics was born as a scientific curiosity in the Victorian age. In 1863, Sir Francis Galton, a cousin of Charles Darwin, theorized that if talented people only married other talented people, the result would be measurably better offspring. At the turn of the last century, Galton's ideas were imported into the United States just as Gregor Mendel's principles of heredity were rediscovered. American eugenic advocates believed with religious fervor that the same Mendelian concepts determining the color and size of peas, corn, and cattle also governed the social and intellectual character of man.

In June 1952, John D. Rockefeller III convened a secret conference at Williamsburg, Virginia, where some thirty of the nation's most eminent conservationists, public health experts, Planned Parenthood leaders, agriculturalists, demographers, and social scientists met. They formed a new group that could act as "a coordinating and catalytic agent in the broad field of population." John D. Rockefeller III publicly christened The Population Council and announced that he himself would serve as its first president. They organized their vast financial and media resources to spread the myth of overpopulation that today is blindly accepted by most as scientific truth. They spread the myth that "people pollute," or as the Rockefeller Foundation's Alan Gregg preferred to describe growing human populations in the developing world, "cancerous growths that demand food." Population reduction became the strategic priority, step-wise, of the US government and then the US-controlled World Bank.

The Rockefeller-financed research into cheap, effective birth control and other eugenics projects resulted in the US government, officially and secretly, making reduction of population growth in key raw material-rich developing countries like Brazil, India, Nigeria, and Indonesia the explicit USA government policy. Henry Kissinger drafted the document for it, NSSM-200, titled, "Implications of Worldwide Population Growth for US Security and Overseas Interests," and President Gerald Ford signed it as government policy in 1975.[78]

In 1957, President Dwight Eisenhower, who warned of a "military-industrial complex," commissioned a panel of scientists to study the issue of overpopulation. The scientists put forth Alternatives I, II, and III that advocate release of deadly viruses and perpetual warfare as means to decrease world population.[79] This supposition dovetails nicely with the pharmaceutical interests of the Rockefellers. According to *Nexus* magazine, the Rockefellers own one-half of the US pharmaceutical industry, which would reap billions developing medicines to "battle" the deadly viruses about to be released. In 1969, the Senate Church Committee discovered that the US Defense Department (DOD) had requested a budget of tens of millions of taxpayer dollars for a program to speed development of new viruses, which target and destroy the human immune system.[80] DOD officials testified before Congress that they planned to produce, "a synthetic biological agent, an agent that does not naturally exist and for which no natural immunity could be acquired and refractory to the immunological and therapeutic processes upon which we depend to maintain our relative freedom from infectious disease."

---

[78] https://en.wikipedia.org/wiki/National_Security_Study_Memorandum_200.

[79] https://www.youtube.com/watch?v=Jib1B2cyWpE.

[80] https://hendersonlefthook.wordpress.com/2014/07/23/the-illuminati-depopulation-agenda/.

Dr. Henry Kissinger wrote: "Depopulation should be the highest priority of US foreign policy towards the Third World."[81] The Rockefeller Foundation helped found the German eugenics program and even funded the program that Josef Mengele worked in before he went to Auschwitz. With the stench of Hitler's mass-murderous frenzy still heavy in the air, Sir Julian Huxley, previously the head of the Eugenics Society, made a smooth transition into pushing world depopulation through UNESCO, whose head he became in 1946, after Hitler's genocide had given eugenics a bad name. Huxley was a fan of Thomas Malthus.

In 1961, Sir Julian Huxley, by then president of the Eugenics Society of Great Britain, in collaboration with Britain's Prince Philip, founded the World Wildlife Fund (WWF), the first president of which was the former card-carrying Nazi, Prince Bernhard of the Netherlands. Bernhard was succeeded in 1976 by John Loudon, the former CEO of Royal Dutch Shell and chairman of Shell Oil Co.

British Royal Consort Prince Philip, who in his interview with *People* magazine, December 21, 1981, said, "We talk about over- and underdeveloped countries; I think a more exact division might be between underdeveloped and overpopulated. The more people there are, the more industry and more waste and the more sewage there is, and therefore the more pollution. Population is a problem."

Prince Phillip, also the cofounder of the World Wildlife Fund, has been a leading organizer of the movement for global depopulation since at least the early 1960s. He's fond of talking of being reincarnated as a "deadly virus" to deal with

---

[81] John Hamer, *The Falsification of History, Our Distorted Reality,* (rossendalebooks.co.uk, 2013), 78.

the population problem. Prince Bernhard of the Netherlands, recently deceased, cofounded the World Wildlife Fund with Philip and used his position to carry out widespread genocide in Africa.[82]

Prince Philip took the helm from 1981 until 1996. Prince Philip, one of the key environmentalist ringleaders throughout the entire post-war period, has provided the world with plenty of evidence indicating his true nature, saying, "You cannot keep a bigger flock of sheep than you are capable of feeding. In other words, conservation may involve culling in order to keep a balance between the relative numbers in each species within any particular habitat. I realize this is a very touchy subject, but the fact remains that mankind is part of the living world. Every new acre brought into cultivation means another acre denied to wild species."[83]

In 1967, Prince Philip, Prince Bernhard, and Maurice Strong formed the secretive 1001 Club to finance the operations of the WWF as well as other covert projects that the WWF was carrying out in Africa. The club comprises members of the most ancient and powerful families of Europe and the British Commonwealth.

Maurice Strong, the top-echelon British-Canadian operative whom we talked about in earlier chapters, was one of the three most influential members, along with Philip and Sir Peter Scott, and has played a critical role over the past forty years in promoting the globalist agenda of world government. From the early 1960s onward, Strong was a friend of, and collaborated closely with, the Rockefeller family, the third generation of which had taken an unusually passionate interest in environmentalism.

---

[82] http://larouchepub.com/eiw/public/2008/2008_40-49/2008_40-49/2008-45/pdf/28-29_4435.pdf.

[83] http://cecaust.com.au/pubs/pdfs/flyer/Pop_Conf_Flyer.pdf.

In 1971, Strong became a trustee of the Rockefeller Foundation, a position he held for many years, guiding the foundation's money in directions he deemed fit.

It was in the early seventies that Henry Kissinger commissioned the murderous 1974 report, National Security Study Memorandum 200, echoing Hitler's words to Lothian by advocating population control in place of industrialization; the report continues even now to be official government policy. National Security Memo 200, dated April 24, 1974, and titled "Implications of worldwide population growth for US security and overseas interests," says: "Dr. Henry Kissinger proposed in his memorandum to the NSC that 'depopulation should be the highest priority of US foreign policy towards the Third World.'"[84] Kissinger cited reasons of national security, and because the US economy will require large and increasing amounts of minerals from abroad, especially from less-developed countries. . . . Wherever a lessening of population can increase the prospects for such stability, population policy becomes relevant to resources, supplies, and to the economic interests of the US.[85]

It was then that anthropologist Margaret Mead started explicitly demanding goals of the environmental movement, including calling for scientists to issue "artificial warnings" that would scare people into adopting conservation and depopulation measures. Using the words of Strong at Stockholm, Margaret Mead told scientists assembled for a 1975 conference on "The Atmosphere: Endangered or Endangering," that the party line was shifting from what scientific analysis had correctly identified

[84] https://en.wikipedia.org/wiki/National_Security_Study_Memorandum_200.
[85] Ibid.

as a process of global cooling, which had begun in the 1940s, to global warming.

In complete disregard for truth and principle, she said,

> The unparalleled increase in the human population and its demands for food, energy, and resources is clearly the most important destabilizing influence in the biosphere. We are facing a period when society must make decisions on a planetary scale. What we need from scientists are estimates, presented with sufficient conservatism and plausibility that will allow us to start building a system of artificial, but effective warnings, warnings which will parallel the instincts of animals which flee the hurricane. [We must] draw from the necessary capacity for sacrifice. It is therefore a statement of major possibilities of danger, which may overtake humankind, on which it is important to concentrate attention.[86]

British Prime Minister Margaret Thatcher was a fanatical Mont Pelerin ideologue whose environmental policies reached across political divides, while one of her top advisors, Sir Crispin Tickell, British ambassador to the UN from 1987–1990 who was the cousin of Aldous Huxley and great-great-grandson of Thomas Huxley, advised Thatcher to promote global warming and population reduction.[87]

Thomas Lovejoy, vice president of the American branch of the World Wildlife Fund (WWF), typified the response of the financiers to this desire in 1984: "The biggest problem is the damn national sectors of these developing countries. These countries think that they have the right to develop their resources as they see fit. They want to become powers."

---

[86] http://www.larouchepub.com/other/2007/sci_techs/3423init_warming_hoax.html.
[87] http://ecofascism.com/review35.html.

With the stock market collapse of 1987, the international financiers were forced to escalate their looting operations to keep the entire monetary system from collapsing. Thatcher organized the Intergovernmental Panel on Climate Change (IPCC) and appointed John Houghton co-chairman. He also held the position of Chairman of Scientific Assessment until 2002. On September 27, 1988, in a speech to the Royal Society of London replete with lies, Thatcher said:

> For generations we have assumed that the efforts of mankind would leave the fundamental equilibrium of the world's systems and atmosphere stable. But it is possible that with all these enormous changes (population, agricultural, use of fossil fuels) concentrated into such a short period of time, we have unwittingly begun a massive experiment with the system of this planet itself. And half the carbon emitted since the Industrial Revolution remains in the atmosphere. We have an extensive research program at our meteorological office for the study of climate change.[88]

At the same time as the launching of the IPCC, Gore, on behalf of and in conjunction with the British Crown, was organizing Global Legislators Organization for a Better Environment (GLOBE). In January 2007, the US Climate Action Partnership (USCAP), a consortium of high-profile corporations (BP, Lehman Brothers, DuPont, GE) and environmentalist groups such as World Resources Institute (WRI), Environmental Defense (ED), and the Natural Resources Defense Council (NRDC), issued a press release supporting GLOBE.

---

[88] http://www.margaretthatcher.org/document/107346.

At one of their events, World Bank President Paul Wolfowitz praised carbon trading, claiming that it could generate as much as $200 billion.

GLOBE was created in 1989 by, primarily, Al Gore and a number of British Parliamentarians. Maurice Strong, who was already a close acquaintance of Gore, told *Executive Intelligence Review* magazine in a 1999 interview that "he [Gore] was very active in the [GLOBE] movement, and, in fact, was instrumental in helping to form [it]. He was the original co-chairman and the driving force in getting it moving. Al was very influential around the world for this."

The key financial affiliations of GLOBE indicate its genocidal and rapacious agenda: the British imperial assets Anglo-American and British Petroleum. The Anglo-Persian Oil Company (APOC) was an English company founded in 1908 following the discovery of a large oil field in Masjed Soleiman, Iran. It was the first company to extract petroleum from Iran. In 1935 APOC was renamed the Anglo-Iranian Oil Company (AIOC) and in 1954 it became the British Petroleum Company (BP), one of the antecedents of the modern BP public limited company. It was in 1992 that Gore published his Malthusian diatribe, *Earth In The Balance: Ecology And The Human Spirit*, known by the short title *Earth in the Balance*. The book explains the world's ecological predicament and describes a range of policies including a proposed "Global Marshall Plan" that includes him advocating dramatic population reduction by as many as two billion.[89]

Depopulation policy became the top priority under the National Security Council (NSC) agenda, Club of Rome, and

---

[89] Al Gore, *Earth in the Balance: Ecology and the Human Spirit*, (Boston, MA: Houghton Mifflin, 1992).

US policymakers like Gen. Alexander Haig, Cyrus Vance, Ed Muskie, and Kissinger. According to an NSC National Security Council spokesman at the time, the United States shared the view of former World Bank President Robert McNamara that the "population crisis" is a greater threat to US national security interests than nuclear annihilation. In 1975, Henry Kissinger established a policy-planning group in the US State Department's Office of Population Affairs. The depopulation "GLOBAL 2000" document for President Jimmy Carter was prepared. It is no surprise that this policy was established under President Carter with help from Kissinger and Brzezinski—all with ties to David Rockefeller. The Bush family, the Harriman family and other partners of Bush in financing Hitler—and the Rockefeller family are the elite of the American eugenics movement.[90] Prescott Bush and other members of the Order Skull & Bones strongly supported Hitler in the period between World Wars I and I. Bush's Union City Bank is known to have funneled many millions of dollars to Hitler's National Socialist Party throughout the 1930's right up until 1942.[91]

Two excellent examples of existing US depopulation policy are first, the long-term impact on the civilian population from Agent Orange in Vietnam, where the Rockefellers built oil refineries and aluminum plants during the Vietnam War. The second is the permanent contamination of the Middle East and Central Asia with depleted uranium, which, unfortunately, will destroy the genetic future of the populations living in those regions and will also have a global effect already reflected in

---

[90] Fritz Springmeier, Bloodlines of the Illuminati, (Portland, OR: Ambassador House, 1999), 428-445, 451.

[91] Anthony Sutton, *America's Secret Establishment: An Introduction to the Order of Skull & Bones,* (Walterville, OR: Trine Day, 2004).

increases in infant mortality reported in the US, Europe, and the UK.

Outspoken depopulation supporter Ted Turner, who has a net worth of $25 billion and is one of the largest US landowners, is one of the most outspoken advocates. In a 2003 interview, the founder of CNN and major United Nations contributor Turner said, "A total population of 250-300 million people, a 95 percent decline would be ideal," as he hailed the efforts of his globalist pal Bill Gates. Bill Gates is the modern day face of eugenics.

Bill Gates has been in the forefront for the depopulation agenda and he publically stated in 2010 during a conference for TED (Technology, Entertainment, and Design) that "The world today has 6.8 billion people . . . that's headed up to about 9 billion. Now if we do a really great job on new vaccines, health care, reproductive health services, we could lower that by perhaps 10 or 15 percent."[92] Take for example, Bill Gates' Polio Vaccine Program. It caused 47,500 cases of paralysis death, and yet he continues to tell the populace we need to reduce population and be vaccinated.

Gates, who is big on mandatory vaccines against pandemics, gives large cash infusions to the CDC, United States Centers for Disease Control and Prevention.

In an article titled, "Study: Polio vaccine campaign in India has caused twelve-fold increase in deadly paralysis condition" by alternative health website naturalnews.com, staff writer Ethan A. Huff reported that:

> The mainstream media has been busy hailing the supposed success of India's polio vaccine campaign over the past few years, with many news outlets now claiming that the disease has been fully eradicated throughout the country. But what

---

[92] https://www.youtube.com/watch?v=Gc16H3uHKOA.

these misinformation puppets are failing to disclose is the fact that cases of non-polio acute flaccid paralysis (NPAFP), a much more serious condition than that caused by polio, have skyrocketed as a result of the vaccine's widespread administration.

What the polio vaccine has done is to increase cases of a more severe condition called non-polio acute flaccid paralysis (NPAFP).

In 2011, for instance, the year in which India was declared to be polio-free, there were 47,500 known cases of NPAFP, which is a shockingly high figure under the circumstances. And based on data collected from India's National Polio Surveillance Project, cases of NPAFP across India rose dramatically in direct proportion to the number of polio vaccines administered, which suggests that the vaccines were responsible for spurring the rapid spread of this deadly condition.

Gates has a penchant for depopulation, a lust for vaccines that knows no bounds and advocates for an extreme Orwellian society that will be monitored and targeted for vaccinations that do more harm than good. Consider what Gates wrote in the *New York Times*.

On March 18, 2015, the king of vaccinations wrote an editorial piece in the *New York Times* in which he speaks about the deadly Spanish Flu and other epidemics that could serve to threaten humanity and he advocates for the United Nations to "fund a global institution" to coordinate the efforts to conduct mass vaccinations. Various global think tank groups legitimize the depopulation agenda in print, as a means to deindustrialize the planet in order to save it from the overuse of fossil fuels.[93]

---

[93] http://www.disclose.tv/forum/the-elite-s-flawed-depopulation-agenda-is-genocide-t98251.html

The depopulation agenda is being legitimized in print by various global think tank groups as a means to deindustrialize the planet in order to save it from the overuse of fossil fuels. Further, the depopulation agenda is being used as an excuse to protect this planet's inhabitants from a dwindling food source. This is one of the biggest lies being perpetrated upon the people. A growing population base is not causing the planet to run out of food.

In 1974, the United Nations organized its first World Population Conference to debate population control. China rolled out its infamous one-child policy in 1980 and this policy was reflective of the founder of Planned Parenthood, Margaret Sanger, when she said, "The most merciful thing that a family does to one of its infant members is to kill it."[94]

In October 2014, the National Academy of Sciences published a shocking report[95] that envisages a Chinese-style global one-child policy as the only means of reversing climate change and reducing global population to a "sustainable" number of one to two billion people. The white paper, entitled Human Population Reduction, is authored by the University of Adelaide's Corey Bradshaw and Barry Brook and presents the impact of world wars and global pandemics that wipe out six billion people as potential methods of combating the "threat posed" to the environment by overpopulation.

The paper is edited by none other than Paul Ehrlich, whom I've mentioned earlier, a perennial advocate of population reduction whose dire and ludicrous proclamations about environmental catastrophes as a result of overpopulation have been proven wildly inaccurate every time. Ehrlich has also

---

[94] U.S. Congress, *Congressional Record.* 111th Cong., Vol. 155, pt. 7, 9251.
[95] http://www.bbc.com/news/science-environment-29788754.

vehemently expressed his support for mandatory population control, arguing that such methods should be imposed and forced if "voluntary methods fail."[96] Ehrlich co-authored *Ecoscience* with Obama's hand-picked science czar John P. Holdren, a book that advocates putting drugs in the water supply to sterilize people, mandatory forced abortions, and a tyrannical eco-fascist dictatorship run by a "planetary regime" and offers a shocking glimpse into the eugenics-driven madness and environmental radicalism that still pervades the halls of academia worldwide.

The United Nations is permeated with individuals who are satanically inspired and have repeatedly, on many fronts, expressed their intent to reduce the world's population by dramatic means, if necessary. Please consider the following quotes:[97]

> The present vast overpopulation, now far beyond the world carrying capacity, cannot be answered by future reductions in the birth rate due to contraception, sterilization and abortion, but must be met in the present by the reduction of numbers presently existing. This must be done by whatever means necessary. – Initiative for the United Nations ECO-92 Earth Charter
>
> One America burdens the earth much more than twenty Bangladesh's. This is a terrible thing to say in order to stabilize world population, we must eliminate 350,000 people per day. It is a horrible thing to say, but it's just as bad not to say it. – Jacques Cousteau, UNESCO Courier

---

[96] Ehrlich, *Population Bomb*.
[97] http://www.thecommonsenseshow.com/2014/04/26/will-humanity-survive-the-depopulation-agenda-of-the-global-elite/.

A reasonable estimate for an industrialized world society at the present North American material standard of living would be 1 billion. At the more frugal European standard of living, 2 to 3 billion would be possible. – United Nations, Global Biodiversity Assessment

War and famine would not do. Instead, disease offered the most efficient and fastest way to kill the billions that must soon die if the population crisis is to be solved. AIDS is not an efficient killer because it is too slow. My favorite candidate for eliminating 90 percent of the world's population is airborne Ebola (Ebola Reston), because it is both highly lethal and it kills in days, instead of years. We've got airborne diseases with 90 percent mortality in humans. Killing humans. Think about that. You know, the bird flu's good, too. For everyone who survives, he will have to bury nine. – Dr. Eric Pianka, at the University of Texas speaking on the topic of reducing the world's population to an audience on population control.

We have to take away from humans in the long run their reproductive autonomy as the only way to guarantee the advancement of mankind. – Francis Crick, the discoverer of the double-helix structure of DNA

Malthus has been vindicated; reality is finally catching up with Malthus. The Third World is overpopulated, it's an economic mess, and there's no way they could get out of it with this fast-growing population. – Dr. Arne Schiotz, World Wildlife Fund Director of Conservation

Society has no business to permit degenerates to reproduce their kind. – Theodore Roosevelt

There is a single theme behind all our work – we must reduce population levels. Either governments do it our way, through nice clean methods, or they will get the kinds of mess that we have in El Salvador, or in Iran or in Beirut.

Population is a political problem. Once population is out of control, it requires authoritarian government, even fascism, to reduce it . . . . Our program in El Salvador didn't work. The infrastructure was not there to support it. There were just too goddamned many people . . . . To really reduce population, quickly, you have to pull all the males into the fighting and you have to kill significant numbers of fertile age females . . . ."[98]

The quickest way to reduce population is through famine, like in Africa, or through disease like the Black Death. – Thomas Ferguson, Latin American State Department Office of Population Affairs

The principle that sustains compulsory vaccination is broad enough to cover cutting the Fallopian tubes. – Justice Oliver Wendell Holmes

The Planetary Regime might be given responsibility for determining the optimum population for the world and for each region and for arbitrating various countries' shares within their regional limits. Control of population size might remain the responsibility of each government, but the Regime would have some power to enforce the agreed limits. – Obama's science czar John P. Holdren from his book, *Ecoscience: Population, Resources, Environment*

Humans have grown like a cancer. We're the biggest blight on the face of the earth. – Ingrid Newkirk, PETA founder, Reader's Digest, 1990

The New World Order elite fully plan to depopulate the planet's six to seven billion people to a manageable level of 500 million as inscribed on the granite monument erected in 1980 in Elbert County, Georgia, called the Georgia Guide-Stones.

---

[98] http://www.thecommonsenseshow.com/2014/04/26/will-humanity-survive-the-depopulation-agenda-of-the-global-elite/.

On these large stones is a message consisting of a set of ten guidelines in eight different languages, one language on each face of the four large upright stones. The first guideline says, "Maintain humanity under 500,000,000 in perpetual balance with nature." There are many full-scale depopulation procedures that have been implemented as population reduction, geo-engineering, land grabs, and criminal banking scams rule the populace. While the global elite construct underground bunkers, eat organic, and hoard seeds in Arctic vaults, the global poor are being slowly starved thanks to high commodity prices and other production limitations. Austerity measures aimed largely at the poor are being imposed on all the nations of the world. The depopulation campaign of the Illuminati is ubiquitously accelerating. The plain and simple truth is that the green agenda is nothing more than a clever global international campaign to eliminate the "useless eaters."

Protecting the environment under the guise of "going green" was simply another means for Gore, Tickell, Maurice Strong, and others, in conjunction with Prince Philip's 1001 Club, to pursue schemes for massive population reduction, all in the tradition of Julian Huxley and the eugenics-loving families of the British Empire and in America. From the late 1980s onward, the British and their global web of agents and organizations have driven the issue of climate change to the forefront of international politics, promoting the pagan doctrine of the Gaia "Mother Earth" cult as a new form of global religion to replace the "outdated" Christian concept of man as made in the creative image of God.

CHAPTER 10

THE HEART OF THE GREEN GOSPEL: GAIA WORSHIP

"What if Mary is another name for Gaia? Then her capacity for virgin birth is no miracle, it is a role of Gaia since life began. She is of this Universe and, conceivably, a part of God. On earth, she is the source of life everlasting and is alive now; she gave birth to humankind and we are part of her."

—Sir James Lovelock, Ages of Gaia

To see the image of Gaia, look no further than your Starbucks coffee cup. Mother Gaia, or Mother Earth, and the Earth Goddess are all the same thing; it is a revival of ancient occult paganism that rejects Christianity. Gaia worship considers Christianity its biggest nemesis and views the Christian faith as its only obstacle to a global religion centered on uniting all life forms around the earth goddess or "Mother Earth." A cunning mixture of science, paganism, eastern mysticism, and feminism has made this pagan green cult of environmentalism the fastest growing religion on the planet and a diabolical emerging threat to the Christian church. It is a fact that Gaia worship is at the very heart of today's environmental policy.

There is a luxuriant oak tree standing just inside the gated entrance of Auschwitz where the sign reads, "Work makes you free." There are many stately oaks inside the camp and just outside the entrance. The gas chamber doors at Auschwitz were made of solid oak. At Auschwitz, double oak doors were used to seal the sacrificial fate of all the victims. Incredibly ironic is that Adolf Eichmann was placed in charge of the logistics of the Holocaust as his last name means "man of the oaks." The ancient symbolism of human sacrifice being practiced under the oak trees bleeds through the Nazi veneer. In fact, the SS letters themselves were iconically stylized after lightning bolts borrowed from nature mystic Guido von List. List promoted a pan-German nature mysticism called Ariosophy, which means "wisdom of the Aryans." It was both anti-modern and anti-Semitic. Ariosophy blended apocalypticism, Norse mythology, paganism, racism, evolution, eugenics, and ecology into its worldview. SS leader Heinrich Himmler was well aware that the Norse god Thor was not only the god of thunder and lightning, but also the god of the oaks. In German paganism, the sacred oak tree symbolized fertility, power, and sacrifice—and sacrifice was the means by which fertility and power were obtained. Sexual fertility and male virility were also symbolized by oaks. Pagan sacrifices were offered in sacred oak groves in order to help guarantee the fertility of nature and her harvest cycles.

The truth is that National Socialism was an ancient fertility cult brought up to date under the scientific guise of eugenics where people were to make sacrifices and be sacrificed for the fecundity of nature. The National Socialists worshipped all fertility, sacrifice, and power. The great desire of National Socialism was to become fertile and powerful through sacrificial eugenic measures.

In his Social Darwinism, Hitler complained that Christianity was itself a "protest against nature," and "the Jew plays in nature the role of a catalyzing element. A people that is rid of its Jews returns spontaneously to the natural order." Indeed, the weaknesses of the modern Western world were presumed to have their crumbling foundations within the longstanding and anti-nature influences of Christianity, which, according to the Nazis, had made Judaism universal.

In his youth, while attending architectural school in Vienna in 1908, Hitler wrote a play about religious sacrifice under massive oaks centering on the differences between Christianity and German paganism witnessed by his roommate August Kubizek. Paganism, oak trees, and human sacrifice hid in the shadows of the firelight blazing around the camp of National Socialism during the Holocaust."[99]

Even the father of deep ecology, Aldo Leopold, complained of America's "Abrahamic" use of the land in his famous book called *The Sand County Almanac* written in 1947. Deep ecology is a contemporary environmental philosophy characterized by its advocacy of the inherent worth of living beings regardless of their instrumental utility to human needs, and advocacy for a radical restructuring of modern human societies in accordance with such ideas.

After the SS tore down Treblinka, lupine wildflowers, which are wolf flowers, were planted on the remains of the Jewish victims where almost 750,000 people were murdered. Hitler

---

[99] Mark Musser, Nazi Oaks, (Altamonte Springs, FL: Advantage Inspirational, 2010).

called the SS his "pack of wolves" and imagined himself as the very Uncle Wolf who would purge the German herd of the weak for the sake of its future eugenic health. On November 3, 1943, some 43,000 Jews were gathered, shot, and killed from various camps in Poland. This concluded Operation Reinhard that had virtually exterminated Polish Jewry. The SS called this final action "Harvest Festival."

The Nazi Party in the 1930s and 40s later absorbed the anti-Semitic historical background of the early German green movement of the 1800s. The greatest crime in the twentieth century, the Holocaust itself, was carried out under a green cover because Nazi racism was largely rooted in Social Darwinism that laid the ecological foundations for what today we know as environmentalism. "This demonstrates the anti-Christian bias of the environmental movement in America, which parallels the anti-Semitic bias in Germany during the 1800s. The Holocaust is best understood as a modernized form of human sacrifice carried out under biological/ecological camouflage that is rooted in the sacrificial oak imagery of ancient paganism. The word *holocaust* itself means "whole burnt offering."[100]

It was the father of German Social Darwinism, Ernst Haeckel, who coined the term *ecology* in 1866. In the early 1900s, Haeckel established the German Monist League, which was one of the first political groups in both racial science and environmentalism. Monism means "one" and many Germans at the time believed that Darwinism established racism as a scientific fact. As such, eugenics became the scientific methodology that was to be used in order to restore humanity's racial evolution that had been compromised by the Christian worldview and its unnatural

---

[100] Ibid.

beliefs and practices. Christianity, they believed, had led the modern world astray, away from the scientific natural laws of evolutionary monism, i.e., racism, which needed to be recovered in order to save Aryan Europe from weakness, overpopulation, and inevitable decline. In those days, German Social Darwinism was called Monism, and many of Germany's early greens were environmental racists and nationalists.

While there were some nuances that distinguished the Monist League from National Socialism, the Nazis drank deeply from Haeckel's Social Darwinism. More than a few Nazis were very attracted to what has to be understood as an early form of environmentalism as well. With the exception of Martin Bormann, all the leading Nazis, including the Führer himself, had their fingers in a piece of the green pie that National Socialism offered to Germany.

As early as 1935, Nazi Germany was far and above the greenest regime on the planet. Eco-fascism is thus no metaphor, but a historical fact. What Marx stated in *Das Kapital* is still held as gospel by his minions today: No one has the right to make a profit off of natural resources, such as food, water, timber, coal, gas, or oil except those who purport to forbid it. And whether it's saving the forests, whales, snails, or the climate, it all comes back to a deep-rooted belief that the quest for such profit is immoral and will ultimately destroy the planet unless ground to a halt. Hitler saw nature, not humankind, as supreme. He also insisted that the environment be protected from commercial development, stating, "Man must not fall into the error of thinking that he was ever meant to become lord and master of nature."

Hitler perceived pollution as the direct result of capitalism and as a fellow materialist who spurned belief in the supernatural, he was completely opposed to the harvesting or mining of natural resources, stating, "The German countryside must be preserved under all circumstances, for it is and has forever been the source of strength and greatness of our people."

Hermann Rauschning, a Danzig Nazi who knew Hitler before and after his accession to power in 1933, tells how in private Hitler acknowledged his profound debt to the Marxist tradition. "I have learned a great deal from Marxism," he once remarked, "as I do not hesitate to admit." He was proud of a knowledge of Marxist texts acquired in his student days before the First World War and later in a Bavarian prison in 1924, after the failure of the Munich putsch. The trouble with Weimar Republic politicians, he told Otto Wagener at much the same time, was that "they had never even read Marx," implying that no one who had failed to read so important an author could even begin to understand the modern world; in consequence, he went on, they imagined that the October revolution in 1917 had been "a private Russian affair," whereas in fact it had changed the whole course of human history!

His differences with the communists, he explained, were less ideological than tactical. German communists he had known before he took power, he told Rauschning, thought politics meant talking and writing. They were mere pamphleteers, whereas "I have put into practice what these peddlers and pen pushers have timidly begun," adding revealingly that "the whole of National Socialism" was based on Marx.

That is a devastating remark and it is blunter than anything in his speeches or in *Mein Kampf*, though even in the autobiography he observes that his own doctrine was fundamentally distinguished from the Marxist doctrine by reason that it recognised the significance of race—implying, perhaps, that it might otherwise easily look like a derivative. Without race, he went on, National Socialism "would really do nothing more than compete with Marxism on its own ground." Marxism was internationalist. The proletariat, as the famous slogan goes, has no fatherland. Hitler had a fatherland, and it was everything to him.

Yet privately, and perhaps even publicly, he conceded that National Socialism was based on Marx. On reflection, it makes consistent sense. The basis of a dogma is not the dogma, much as the foundation of a building is not the building, and in numerous ways National Socialism was based on Marxism.

One of the original gurus who championed the cause of environmentalism over national security concerns was German green activist Dr. Erich Hornsmann. In postwar West Germany, Hornsmann often complained that the destruction of Mother Nature was "Enemy Number One." In 1947, Hornsmann became a founding member of the Protection of German Forests. In 1955, he wrote *The Forest: The Foundation of our Existence*. He warned of spreading desertification problems associated with the cutting down of trees and expanding ski resorts on mountain slopes. Dr. Hornsmann even led the postwar charge on promoting radical water conservation measures. Hornsmann also belonged to the Alliance for the Protection of German Waters and wrote extensively on how water was becoming an increasingly scarce commodity. Hornsmann applied Malthusian math to the waters of Germany as he was convinced that water consumption would outstrip water supplies as personal usage of it skyrocketed with ever-increasing showers and baths. Hornsmann also wrote an apocalyptic environmental book entitled *Otherwise*

Collapse: The Answer of the Earth to the Abuse of Her Laws.
To counteract the green catastrophe looming just around the
corner, Hornsmann was convinced that environmental land use
planning was absolutely required to avoid doomsday. Much of
the apocalyptic environmentalism so rampant in today's political
world goes back to Germany and rabid environmentalists like
Dr. Hornsmann.

Modern environmentalism is largely rooted in Germany
like a giant oak tree that tapped into German Existentialism
and Social Darwinism and flowered in the European continent
throughout the 1800s—all of which value nature over people
and laid the foundation of today's green movement. There are
two major engines driving the new world green agenda: a quest
for control and its adoption as a fundamental religious belief.
What makes this paradigm so perilous and effective is that it
merges both forces together under the seemingly benevolent,
but malevolent goal of "taking care of the environment." The
"Mother Gaia needs protection" mantra is woven throughout
all of the major initiatives, forums, and organizations of the
sustainable development agenda. To begin to understand the
purported reasons behind the agenda for a new world order
and a new world religion, it is critical to investigate the religious
beliefs of the organizations and individuals behind it, and
how those convictions undergird an agenda of control. This
religious conviction and political agenda of control are shared
by, according to many accounts, the most powerful man in the
world, Maurice Strong. Maurice Strong was Secretary General
of the UN's Rio Earth Summit in 1992 (where Agenda 21
was adopted) and former Executive Director and founder of
United Nations Environment Program (UNEP). Henry Lamb

of Sovereignty International, Tennessee, a UN-accredited Non-governmental Organization (NGO), said in a 2012 interview just three months before his death, "Strong is perhaps more than any other single person, responsible for the development of a global agenda now being implemented throughout the world." Strong, a billionaire and influential UN bureaucrat, is a devotee of the Gaia movement. "He's the most dangerous man in the world," said Tom DeWeese, founder of the American Policy Center, Virginia, a conservative think tank. "At the United Nations, all roads lead to him."

To help illuminate the scope of Strong's influence, consider that he has served in a multitude of key international positions, including Director of the World Economic Forum Foundation, Chairman of the Earth Council, Chairman of the Stockholm Environment Institute, Senior Advisor to the president of the World Bank, Chairman of the World Resources Institute, and most interestingly, Finance Director at the Temple of Understanding (TOU). Strong and his wife created a foundation in 1988 "to provide land and financial support to qualified spiritual organizations, earth stewardship programs, and related educational opportunities for youth and adults," according to the Crestone Institute. Their 200,000-acre ranch near Crestone, Colorado, known as Baca Grande, is now a new age spiritual center run by Strong's wife.

Maurice Strong, the high priest of humanism, launched the Earth Charter Initiative in 1994. In 1997, the Earth Council and Green Cross International formed an Earth Charter Commission to give oversight to the process. Strong co-founded the Earth Charter with Mikhail Gorbachev in 1997, and it has been endorsed by the UN and reveals the spiritual nature of the agenda for sustainable development.

In its preamble, the Earth Charter states,

> We must join together to bring forth a sustainable global society founded on respect for nature, universal human rights, economic justice, and a culture of peace . . . . The protection of earth's vitality, diversity, and beauty is a sacred trust.

After addressing the fact that "the benefits of development are not shared equitably . . ." the communist principle of redistribution of wealth from the haves to the have-nots, the preamble goes on to express:

> The emergence of a global civil society is creating new opportunities to build a democratic and humane world. Our environmental, economic, political, social, and spiritual challenges are interconnected, and together we can forge inclusive solutions . . . . The spirit of human solidarity and kinship with all life is strengthened when we live with reverence for the mystery of being, gratitude for the gift of life, and humility regarding the human place in nature.

Strong's comments in his opening address at the Rio Earth Summit summarize his philosophy clearly: "It is the responsibility of each human today to choose between the force of darkness and the force of light . . . . We must therefore transform our attitudes, and adopt a renewed respect for the superior laws of divine nature."

On September 9, 2001, a creation celebration of the Earth Charter was held at Shelburne Farms in Vermont for the unveiling of the Earth Charter's final resting place. An "Ark of Hope" was presented to the United Nations, along with its contents, in June of 2002. Placed within the Ark, along with the Earth Charter, were various items called "Temenos Books" and "Temenos Earth Masks." Temenos is a concept adopted by Carl Jung to denote a magic circle, a sacred space where special rules and energies apply. Children, who filled them with visual affirmations for Mother Earth, created some of the Temenos Books within this magic circle. Fashioned with the "earth elements," the Temenos Earth Masks were also worn and created by children. In the words of Steven W. Mosher, president of Population Research Institute, "Gaia is the New Age term for Mother Earth. The New Age believers hold that the earth is a sentient super-being, a kind of goddess, deserving of worship and, some say, human sacrifice. Compared to Gaia worship, the simple animism of primitive cultures is wholesome."

Inside the "Ark of Hope," the Earth Charter was handwritten on papyrus paper and ready for presentation to the United Nations. Each panel of the Ark of Hope contained one of the five traditional elements of pagan worship: water, fire, earth, air, and spirit. According to the Ark of Hope website, the Ark's dimensions are 49" × 32" × 32" and it was crafted out of a single sycamore plank. The obvious meaning behind the Ark of Hope is that it is a mockery of God's Ten Commandments and the Ark of the Covenant. In this context, the choice of sycamore wood for the Ark of Hope's construction is a revealing one. The sycamore tree was sacred to most all the pagan religions in the Middle East during biblical times, and in Egypt especially, burial in sycamore coffins was a symbolic return into the womb of the mother goddess.

The Rockefeller Foundation and a new age organization called the Lindisfarne Institute, of which Maurice Strong is also a member, generously sponsor these pagan festivals in a supposedly Christian church. This practice of using the sites or structures of previous beliefs is common throughout history as a sign of new order and dominance. The adoption and adaptation of Christian terms and symbols, like "Ark of the Covenant," achieves the same objective.

One of the most influential NGOs (non-governmental organizations) allied closely with the UN is the Temple of Understanding (TOU), located in the Cathedral of St. John the Divine in New York City. According to its website, this organization's objectives are "developing an appreciation of religious and cultural diversity, educating for global citizenship and sustainability, expanding public discourse on faith and ecology, and creating just and peaceful communities." This cathedral is the center of cosmology, or the worship of Gaia. The Cathedral of St. John the Divine is not only home to the TOU, but it also previously housed the National Religious Partnership for the Environment, the Lindisfarne Association, and the Gaia Institute, which are all proponents of the Gaia hypothesis. Among its many globally influential board of directors members is the Reverend Thomas Berry, the most prominent evangelist for the Gaia hypothesis. The *Wanderer Forum Quarterly* describes the man's religious philosophy:

> Thomas Berry, Catholic Priest, claims that it is now time for the most significant change that Christian spirituality has yet experienced. This change is part of a much more comprehensive change in human consciousness brought about by the discovery of the evolutionary story of the universe. In speaking about a new cosmology he reminds us that we are the earth come to consciousness and, therefore, we are connected to the whole living community—that is,

all people, animals, plants, and the living organism of planet earth itself.

In Berry's own words, according to the *Florida Catholic* (February 14, 1992),

> We must rethink our ideas about God; we should place less emphasis on Christ as a person and redeemer. We should put the Bible away for twenty years while we radically rethink our religious ideas. What is needed is the change from an exploitative anthropocentrism to a participative biocentrism. This change requires something more than environmentalism.

Gaia has become much more than simply a scientific hypothesis; it has transformed into a fervent religious movement that is the driving force behind global social change.

The "Gaia hypothesis" can be credited to James Lovelock. Lovelock worked for NASA during the 1960s as a consultant to the "life on Mars" Viking spacecraft project. Lovelock's theory claimed that the earth's "biota," (biota are the total collection of organisms of a geographic region or a time period, from local geographic scales and instantaneous temporal scales all the way up to whole-planet and whole-timescale spatiotemporal scales) tightly coupled with its environment, acts as a single, self-regulating living system in such a way as to maintain the conditions suitable for life. According to Lovelock, this living system was the result of a meta-life form that occupied our planet billions of years ago and began a process of transforming this planet into its own substance. He claimed that all of the life forms on this planet are a part of Gaia—a spirit goddess that sustains life on earth. Since this transformation into a living system, he theorizes, the interventions of Gaia have brought about the evolving diversity of living creatures on planet earth. From Lovelock's perspective in space, he saw not a planet, but a self-evolving and self-regulating living system. His theory presented earth not as the rock that it is, but as a living being and fount of all life. He named this living being Gaia, after the Greek goddess that was once believed to have drawn the living world forth from Chaos.

The idea of earth as a living, divine spirit is not a new one. Plato said, "We shall affirm that the cosmos, more than anything else, resembles most closely that living Creature of which all other living creatures, severally or genetically, are portion; a living creature which is fairest of all and in ways most perfect."

As today's updated version of paganism, Gaia is eagerly accepted by the new age movement and fits neatly into eastern mysticism, but it needed an infusion of science to gather in the evolutionists and science-minded humanists. For these people, Gaia was made palatable by Lovelock's Daisyworld model, a mathematical and scientific theory designed to refute the criticisms of Darwin's groupies. Just as evolution eliminates the need for a divine creator, the Daisyworld model provided a theory of evolving life on earth that incorporates natural selection with a world that is interconnected. It eliminates a personal yet separate God and makes humans a part of the divine spirit that is Gaia. According to the report, Lovelock said, "She is of this universe and, conceivably, a part of God. On earth she is the source of life everlasting and is alive now; she gave birth to humankind and we are a part of her." The report indicates that Lovelock ". . . likened the current global warming to the first signs of a fever," but is worried that "we are not allowing Gaia to recuperate." In other words, earth, as one huge organism, is seen as one with God. By doing damage to the earth, humans are, according to this belief, damaging God. It is this spiritual conviction that provides the rabid determination behind the environmental movement and the objectives of sustainable development.

It is interesting to note that in April of 2012 James Lovelock admitted that his previous claims were "alarmist." The ninety-two-year-old said climate change is still happening—just not as quickly as he once warned. He added that other environmental commentators, such as former Vice President Al Gore, are also guilty of exaggerating their arguments. The admission came as a devastating blow to proponents of climate change who hailed Lovelock as a powerful figurehead for their hype. Lovelock, who once reported, "Before this century is over billions of us will die and the few breeding pairs of people that survive will be in the Arctic where the climate remains tolerable," admitted to MSNBC that he "made a mistake" and further went on to say, "We don't know what the climate is doing—we thought we knew twenty years ago but the temperature has stayed almost constant, whereas it should have been rising—carbon dioxide is rising, no question about that."

More appealing to the New Agers, evolutionists, science-minded humanists, and the interfaith movement is the mystical side of Gaia. They can easily relate to the belief that humans can have mystical experiences or a spiritual relationship with Gaia. A connectedness to nature and the belief that humans are a part of this collective consciousness called Gaia appeals to them. Gaia teaches that an "Earth Spirit," goddess, or planetary brain must be protected. It is this belief that fuels the environmental movement, sustainable development, and the global push for the return of industrialized nations to a more primitive way of life. Just as with the evolutionists, the humanists, and the other pagan religions of the world, Gaia has named Christianity as the obstacle to human evolution and our spiritual destiny. A document mandated by the UN-sponsored Convention on Biological Diversity, the Global Biodiversity Assessment, explicitly refers to Christianity as a faith that has set humans apart from nature and stripped nature of its sacred qualities. The document states:

> Conversion to Christianity has therefore meant an abandonment of an affinity with the natural world for many forest dwellers, peasants, fishers all over the world . . . . The northeastern hilly states of India bordering China and Myanmar supported small scale, largely autonomous shifting cultivator societies until the 1950s. These people followed their own religious traditions that included setting apart between 10 percent and 30 percent of the landscape as sacred groves and ponds.

While condemning Christianity as the root of all ecological evil, the document goes on to praise Buddhism and Hinduism as they "did not depart as drastically from the perspective of humans as members of a community of beings including other living and non-living elements." The global government favors non-Christian religions as good stewards of Mother Earth. To help illuminate the beliefs of Gaia, as propagated by the Temple of Understanding (TOU) and many UN leaders and organizations behind this new world order agenda, it is helpful to review a UN report called Shared Vision, from the 1988 Global Forum of

Spiritual and Parliamentary Leaders for Human Survival, which was founded by the Temple of Understanding. In summarizing the speech given at the conference, Lovelock's contribution is to suggest that life on earth regulates its environment as if it were one huge organism. The name given to the organism—and the idea—is that of Gaia, the Greek earth goddess.

The 1988 Global Forum of Spiritual and Parliamentary Leaders for Human Survival began the marriage between religion and environmental objectives on a worldwide scale. From this conference, many additional forums around the world were organized to bring together the world leaders in government, environment, religion, and science for the purpose of collaborating on the goals of sustainable development. The National Religious Partnership for the Environment (NRPE), created in 1993, came out of these global meetings. The NRPE developed a plan for "integrating issues of social justice and the environment," which included education and action kits to religious congregations around the world, training programs for religious students and leaders, and a variety of other worldwide actions specifically designed to ensure that religious groups stringently adopted their globalist environmental agenda goals. Worldwide religion, the objectives of sustainable development, and the Gaia movement all became woven together into a tapestry of broad-scale worldwide control.

Blending the world's religions together and bringing them under the umbrella of the United Nations has been high on the global green agenda for many years. Dr. Robert Muller is one of the key people who are the driving force behind the plan to create a new united religion. Muller spent fifty-three years working within the United Nations and was the Assistant

Secretary-General for more than twelve years. He is the Founder and Chancellor of the United Nations University of Peace. Here is how he describes himself: "A divine motivator . . . the wise man of the UN . . . the shaman of the UN . . . the man through whom God speaks . . . the spokesman of Christ . . . a magic being . . . ."

Muller was a key architect behind many of the UN's most important environmental policies and plans. Let's take a look at some of Muller's quotes:

> Hindus call our earth Brahma, or God, for they rightly see no difference between our earth and the divine. This ancient simple truth is slowly dawning again upon humanity, as we are about to enter our cosmic age and become what we were always meant to be: the planet of god.
>
> What an incredible planet in the universe this will be when we will be one human family living in justice, peace, love, and harmony with our divine earth, with each other, and with the heavens.

Muller, who was the right-hand man to three consecutive UN Secretary Generals and was responsible for formulating many UN policies and programs, clearly believes that the earth is divine. He describes conversations between himself and God, and between himself and the earth. In one article, Muller recounts a conversation between himself and God as equals, no less. Here is what Muller recounts:

> God: Dear Robert, I congratulate you for having finished your 4,000 ideas. May I ask you which one do you consider most important, my most important?

Muller: In conclusion after all my adult life as civil servant is that the United Nations must be vastly strengthened to resolve major global problems—it must be empowered to adopt and enforce world laws and regulations. Let us perform this miracle in the house of Mica on the shores of the River of the Rising Sun where from our indigenous brethren prophesied that a civilization of peace will extend to the entire world.

God: Thank you, dear Robert, for what you are recommending. Perhaps after all the greatest jewel of my creation, the earth, can be saved.

A group of interfaith dialogue proponents decided to organize a centennial conference to be held in 1993. Dr. Muller was one of the primary organizers, along with Hans Kung and with Dr. Gerald Barney as a keynote speaker. Kung is a Catholic priest who previously held the powerful position of Expositor of Theology at the Vatican and is the founder of the Global Ethic Foundation, an organization strongly pushing the concept of human global consciousness.

The conference included more than 8,000 representatives from 150 different religious and spiritual groups. Dr. Muller's speech was entitled "A Proposal to Establish the United Nations of Religion." The centenary parliament led to the formation of interfaith dialogue initiatives by many religious groups, most notably the Vatican and the United Nations, the Gorbachev Foundation, the Clinton Global Initiative, and many UN-associated NGOs. However, it was the United Religions Initiative (URI) proposed by Robert Muller during the conference that has made the most dramatic progress. The URI's stated aims are "unity amongst religions" and "manifesting love for the earth." Working closely with Muller on this initiative was the Anglican Bishop William Swing of Grace Episcopal Cathedral in San Francisco.

Although Muller is the visionary behind United Religions and the catalyst between the major parties involved, Swing has become the initiative's figurehead and spokesperson. The URI claims that more than 1,000 religious groups representing 600 million people have endorsed the URI charter. These include the Dalai Lama, state churches in China, various Jewish rabbis, Sufis, a Muslim sect, the Rev. Sun Myung Moon, radical feminists, deep ecologists, creation spiritualists, kabbalists, and various neo-pagan groups. It has also received favorable comments from the United Nations and the Vatican. The preamble to the URI's stated aims are as follows:

> We people of diverse religions, spiritual expressions, and indigenous traditions throughout the world hereby establish the United Religions Initiative to promote in enduring daily interphase cooperation to end religiously motivated violence and create cultures of peace, justice, and healing for the earth and all living beings. We unite to heal and protect the earth.

The charter goes on to say the "root of this ecological crisis is a spiritual crisis."

The United Nations has granted the URI official liaison status, which means that in return for UN financial support the URI will cooperate closely with the UN.

Bishop Swing issued a challenge for a new global civilization at a UN-sponsored interfaith conference where he said: "We stand on the threshold of a new world order that may be defined either by an increasing polarization that fuels a spiral of escalating conflict or by growing global cooperation that calls the human race to work across religious boundaries to serve a larger global good."

Swing went on to say that he regretted proclaiming that Jesus Christ is Lord and Savior of all and seeking to make the whole world Christian. He said this "because someday, the ascendancy of militant fundamentalist voices of politically aspiring religions might be so pervasive that a united religion will need to be created in order to save religions from these fundamentalists." Swing said,

> The United Religions Initiative is intended to be to religion what the United Nations has become to global politics, unifying the world's religions as the UN is unifying the world's nations. The URI will offer the world a powerful new vision of hope—the vision that the deepest stories we know can now cease to be causes of separation between people, and become instead the foundation for a reunited humanity. The URI, in time, aspires to have the visibility and stature of the United Nations. It will have global visibility and will be a vital presence in local communities all over the world. The URI will be a spiritual United Nations.

Reverend James Davis, an Anglican minister from New York, stated, "We've never seen any organization build coalitions as quickly or as successfully as the United Religions Initiative."[101] Huston Smith, a scholar of comparative religions and author of *The World's Religions*, a standard reference in religious studies, describes the URI as "by far the most significant global interfaith effort."[102]

---

[101] https://agendatwentyone.wordpress.com/category/spirituality/.
[102] http://www.green-agenda.com/unitedfaith.html

Dr. Muller gives evidence to the marriage of Gaia with the movement of sustainable development in his paper "A Cosmological Vision of the Future" (1989):

> Now we're learning that perhaps this planet has not been created for humans, but that humans have been created for the planet . . . . We are living earth. Each of us is a cell, a perceptive nervous unit of the earth. The living consciousness of the earth is beginning to operate through us . . . . We have now a world brain which determines what can be dangerous or mortal for the planet: the United Nations and its agencies, and innumerable groups and networks around the world, are part of the brain. This is our newly discovered meaning . . . . we are a global family living in a global home. We are in the process of becoming a global civilization . . . . The third millennium should be a spiritual millennium, a millennium which will see the integration and harmony of humanity with creation, with nature, with the planet, with the cosmos, and with eternity.

This key UN leader, in charge of creating worldwide policy, goes on to highlight how cosmological faith drives an agenda for a global community, "in the interest of protecting the goddess of nature." Muller won the UNESCO Prize in 1989 for Peace Education for his World Core Curriculum, an educational initiative to turn students into global citizens who put the planet first. According to Muller's website, "The entire humanity must be reprogrammed through a UN-endorsed global education." Muller explained the reasons behind his World Core Curriculum in a 1995 speech to the College of Law at the University of Denver:

> I've come to the conclusion that the only correct education that I have received in my life was from the United Nations.

We should replace the word politics by planetics. We need planetary management, planetary caretakers. We need global sciences. We need a science of a global psychology, a global sociology, a global anthropology.

Muller's influential philosophy is the perfect example of how a pantheistic nature-centered spirituality and an agenda of worldwide control go hand in hand with the United Nations and its supporting organizations.

Al Gore is also a big fan of Muller's concepts. Gore is now the secular high priest for Gaia and a radical devotee of pantheism as the poster boy and modern face of the environmental movement. Gore has been involved with the Temple of Understanding, including giving a sermon at its annual celebration of St. Francis, a ceremony who's Blessing of the Animals included blessings for an elephant, algae, and a bowl of worms and compost. According to a 1994 publication by the Cathedral at St. John the Divine, Gore gave a sermon where he asserted, "God is not separate from the earth." Gore's book *Earth in the Balance* has three chapters devoted to the "Earth Goddess" and he writes, "This we know: the earth does not belong to man, man belongs to the earth. All things are connected like the blood that unites us all." Gaia's holy warrior goes on to echo the view that

Prehistoric Europe and much of the world was based on the worship of a single earth goddess, who was assumed to be the fount of all life and who radiated harmony among all living things. Much of the evidence for the existence of this primitive religion comes from the many thousands of artifacts uncovered in ceremonial sites. These sites are so widespread that they seem to confirm the notion that a goddess religion was ubiquitous through much of the world until the antecedents of today's religions, most of which still have a distinctly masculine orientation . . . swept out of India and the Near East, almost obliterating belief in the goddess. The last vestige of organized goddess worship was eliminated by Christianity as late as the fifteenth century in Lithuania.

Gore then quotes de Chardin, "The fate of mankind, as well as of religion, depends upon the emergence of a new faith in the future. Armed with such a faith, we might find it possible to resanctify the earth . . . ."

Gore is also very fond of frequently quoting an old North American Indian saying, "Will you teach your children what we have taught our children? That the earth is our Mother? What befalls the earth, befalls all the sons of the earth. This we know—the earth does not belong to man, man belongs to the earth."

It is important that you realize that Gaia worship is at the very heart of the Global Green Agenda. Sustainable Development, Agenda 21, the Earth Charter, and the man-made global warming hysteria are all part and parcel of the Gaians' mission to save "Mother Earth" from her human infestation. These Gaia-loving occultists have succeeded in uniting the environmental movement, the new age movement, Eastern religions, the United Nations, and even the leaders of many Christian denominations behind this vile form of paganism that dates back to the druids. The can has a new label, but its contents are the same. The theme repeats itself: A pantheistic, new age belief that the earth is goddess Gaia and humanity is here to protect Gaia above all else, no matter what the cost.

The United Nations Global Biodiversity Assessment explicitly refers to Christianity as a faith that has set humans apart from nature and stripped nature of its sacred qualities. Christianity therefore has to be eradicated as it diametrically opposes the Gaians' love for the natural world. While condemning Christianity as the root of all environmental evil, the document goes on to praise Buddhism and Hinduism. Members of this "Green Religion" all agree that the earth is in a crisis state and this ecological emergency is the result of Christian traditions. They believe that the Judeo-Christian belief that God assigned man to rule over the earth has caused us to exploit and abuse it. Monotheism, they assert, has separated humans from their ancient connection to the earth and to reverse this trend, governments, the media, our education system, and other areas of influence must revive and reconnect us to earth's spirit.

If Gore had read the Bible, he would know exactly why Christians will not open their minds to these other beliefs as he suggests. The Bible very clearly warns us not to.

> So then, just as you received Christ Jesus as Lord, continue to live in him, rooted and built up in him, strengthened in the faith as you were taught, and overflowing with thankfulness. See to it that no one takes you captive through hollow and deceptive philosophy, which depends on human tradition and the basic principles of this world rather than on Christ. For in Christ all the fullness of the Deity lives in bodily form, and you have been given fullness in Christ, who is the head over every power and authority.
>
> (Col. 2:6-10 NIV)

Gore also might want to read Romans 1:18-25:

For the wrath of God is revealed from heaven against all ungodliness and unrighteousness of men, who hold the truth in unrighteousness;

Because that which may be known of God is manifest in them; for God hath shewed it unto them.

For the invisible things of him from the creation of the world are clearly seen, being understood by the things that are made, even his eternal power and Godhead; so that they are without excuse:

Because that, when they knew God, they glorified him not as God, neither were thankful; but became vain in their imaginations, and their foolish heart was darkened.
Professing themselves to be wise, they became fools,

And changed the glory of the uncorruptible God into an image made like to corruptible man, and to birds, and four-footed beasts, and creeping things.

Wherefore God also gave them up to uncleanness through the lusts of their own hearts, to dishonour their own bodies between themselves:

Who changed the truth of God into a lie, and worshipped and served the creature more than the Creator, who is blessed forever.

When men began to worship the creation instead of the Creator, the wrath of God was revealed. As societies begin again to turn from the truth of the creation and worship nature, Mother Earth, or any other deceiving spirit, the evil and deception in their new religion will be made evident by God's response. Our society today has becoming a picture of this wickedness, evil, greed, and depravity. As the Christian church is brought into the fold by organizations such as the National Council of Churches and the National Religious Partnership for the Environment, we can be sure the results will be a further decline into immorality and chaos. There is a drive by these organizations and others to meld earth worship with Christianity in the name of tolerance, biodiversity, sustainability, and the preservation of Mother Gaia.

It is a battle for Christianity and an attack on biblical truth. This pagan agenda will reach your church, if it hasn't yet. It is important for Christians to speak up for the truth of God and not exchange the glory of the living God for a global compromise that is leading countless people into spiritual darkness.

As followers of Jesus Christ, we know the truth and must boldly proclaim it. The opposition is fierce and to those who don't know the joy of a relationship with God, it is an appealing proposition. It is accepting of everything, intolerant of nothing, it deifies the environmentalist, worships the feminist, eliminates all responsibility for sin, and frees you to embrace your sinful nature.

The truth of the Bible must first be taught in our churches and then shared with the world. As churches begin to fall away from the faith, corrupt the Word of God, and water down the Gospel of Jesus Christ, it is left to Spirit-filled, Bible-believing Christians to stand up for the truth, contend for our faith, and offer to the world an alternative to God's wrath. If we are ashamed of our faith, if we compromise our beliefs, and if we hide in our churches and ignore what is going on outside of them, we are aiding in our own destruction and countless souls will be lost because of our complacency, selfishness, and inaction.

Because of this, God gave them over to shameful lusts. Even their women exchanged natural relations for unnatural ones.

In the same way the men also abandoned natural relations with women and were inflamed with lust for one another. Men committed indecent acts with other men, and received in themselves the due penalty for their perversion. Furthermore, since they did not think it worthwhile to retain the knowledge of God, he gave them over to a depraved mind, to do what ought not to be done. They have become filled with every kind of wickedness, evil, greed and depravity. They are full of envy, murder, strife, deceit and malice. They are gossips, slanderers, God-haters, insolent, arrogant and boastful; they invent ways of doing evil; they disobey their parents; they are senseless, faithless, heartless, and ruthless. Although they know God's righteous decree that those who do such things deserve death, they not only continue to do these very things but also approve of those who practice them.

(Rom. 1:26-32 NIV)

In previous chapters we discussed the First Global Revolution and outlined how the very influential members of the "Club of Rome" have decided that the earth is facing an "imminent ecological collapse" and drastic measures must be taken immediately to save Gaia from the destructive beast of capitalism. They claimed that a new enemy was required in order to unite humanity, "one either real or invented for the purpose," and that "the threat of global warming" is the ideal crisis. To Gaians, who see earth as Gaia and speak of "her" as a real living sentient earth-spirit, the theory of global warming presents a dream scenario. It strikes at the very heart of "Gaia's greatest threat"—capitalism and modern industrial society. According to them, without fossil fuels, the world will be transformed into the Gaians' ecotopian vision of small sustainable human settlements surrounded by protected wild-lands, governed by some United Earth Council. Global warming provides a clarion call to which the green masses can rally. Skeptics are now demonized as climate deniers and climate criminals, insinuating that they should be locked up and done away with. Al Gore's compatriot, David Suzuki, has called for eco police to be implemented with stiff punishments for deniers.

Many of the most vocal politicians and scientists of the green movement actively and vocally espouse their neopaganism philosophy when insisting that humans are the cause of global warming. There is always a key theme to their ranting—global transformation.

So what is this new cult of Gaia? It is a rehashed, modernized version of the paganism condemned by God in the Bible. Science, evolution theory, and a space age mentality have given it a new face and made it sound more trendy and sexy to the modern world, but it is the same paganism in all of its evils. There is undoubtedly a link between Gaia, global warming, and global governance, and the three are wrapped and tied with a big green bow.

It becomes evident that the global transformationalists are promoting the Green Gospel as the "new scripture." This is not simply an idealistic agenda, but a deeply rooted spiritual belief about nature as god. It is a growing and expanding agenda, driven by religious conviction and intricately interconnected with a plan for a tightly controlled global society. And it is a plan that is being propagated by the most influential individuals and organizations on the planet.

Professing themselves to be wise, they became fools. And changed the glory of the uncorruptible God into an image made like corruptible man, and to birds, and four-footed beasts, and creeping things. Wherefore God also gave them up to uncleanness, through the lusts of their own hearts, to dishonour their own bodies between themselves: Who changed the truth of God into a lie, and worshipped and served the creature more than the Creator, who is blessed forever. Amen.

(Rom. 1:22-25 KJV)

CHAPTER 11

POPE FRANCIS: THE PATRON SAINT OF THE ENVIRONMENT & HIS GREEN THEOLOGY

In 1990, John Paul II said Catholics had a special religious obligation to protect God's creation from damage caused by "industrial waste, the burning of fossil fuels, unrestricted deforestation" and other practices. Pope Benedict XVI was dubbed "the Green Pope" for his frequent calls to stop ecological devastation and his efforts to bring solar power to the Vatican city. He asked, "Can we remain indifferent before the problems associated with such realities as climate change?"

Following the resignation of Pope Benedict XVI on February 28, 2013, a papal conclave elected Jorge Marion Bergoglio as his successor on March 13, 2013. Clearly, the unprecedented papal-switch of 2013 that saw Benedict step down and Bergoglio step in, reportedly took his papal title after St. Francis of Assisi of Italy, founder of the Franciscan order of the Friars Minor. Like Hitler, St. Francis of Assisi was a devout "admirer of nature." St. Francis also gave up his considerable wealth following an illness that took him near to death. Pope Francis took his name because he also admires the rejection of wealth and redistribution of wealth in the socialist manner. Francis is actually the first Jesuit Pope. The Jesuits were formed by Ignatius Loyola to act as the strict upholders of religious law, which puts many of Pope Francis's ideas in conflict with Catholic teaching. Within the Roman Catholic Church, there are two types of priests: the secular clergy and those who are part of religious orders. The first group are known as diocesan priests, and will often (though not always) be attached to a parish and are accountable to a local bishop. They train at a seminary, a theological college, and do not take vows of poverty or seclude themselves from the outside world. In many ways they are the public face of the Catholic Church. Religious orders, by contrast, have more autonomy from the central church. They are not under the jurisdiction of a bishop (who in turn has been appointed by the pope) and can live completely excluded from secular society, depending on the order they belong to. Monks and friars—such as the Dominicans, Benedictines, Cistercians (including Trappists) and Franciscans—live within their orders, though often will be connected to educational institutions and can run select parishes. In Britain alone the Benedictines teach at Ampleforth College, a public school in north England, while the Dominicans run Blackfriars Hall, an Oxford college.[103]

Coercion of the Pope to embrace the global warming message likely began with John Kerry's visit to the Vatican in January 2014 ostensibly to discuss Middle East issues. The *Boston Globe* researched Kerry during his presidential run and discovered that the Kerry family was traced back to a small town in the Austrian empire, now part of the Czech Republic. There, the paper

---

[103] http://www.economist.com/blogs/newsbook/2013/03/economist-explains-who-are-jesuits-exactly

discovered, before emigrating to America, the family changed their name from Kohn to Kerry and converted from Judaism to Catholicism. His Catholicism caused him much political trouble during his presidential campaign.

Now the Obama administration has taken the next step, which is standard in the entire development of the Intergovernmental Panel on Climate Change (IPCC) climate campaign, by involving the top bureaucrat of the Environmental Protection Agency (EPA), Gina McCarthy. Gina McCarthy says her goal is to show the Vatican how aligned President Barack Obama and Francis are on climate change. "Global warming isn't just an environmental issue, but a public health threat, and yet also a chance for economic opportunity." Her comment eerily parallels the political objective identified by Canadian Environment Minister Christine Stewart, who said, "No matter if the science of global warming is all phony . . . climate change provides the greatest opportunity to bring about justice and equality in the world."

Consider Nazi collaborator and racist advocate of mass genocide Prince Philip, a man who as I have previously stated, has often expressed his desire to return to the earth as a "deadly virus" to thin the human population and who says that there are too many people in the world, was quoted by the BBC Saying "the growing human population was the biggest challenge to conservation and 'voluntary family limitation' was the only way to tackle it."[104]

Religious and political analogies abound between environmentalism and its subset, global warming. Former Czech Republic President Vaclav Klaus, who gave the keynote address

---

[104] http://www.bbc.com/news/uk-13682432.

at the first Heartland Climate Conference in New York, warned about the growing trend. "There is another threat on the horizon. I see this threat in environmentalism, which is becoming a new dominant ideology, if not a religion. Its main weapon is raising the alarm and predicting the human life-endangering climate change based on man-made global warming."

Proponents of the IPCC and their anthropogenic global warming (AGW) hypothesis continue their crusade (pun intended) by inveigling the support of authority figures like the Pope and by inference, associated groups.

These are classic appeals to authority, like Lord May's use of the Royal Society to persuade other science societies to support the AGW cause. Most members of the Society didn't know what their leaders were doing and many demanded a retraction or at least a restatement.

The Pope apparently did not think through his commitment to the IPCC claims as expounded by the Obama White House. Likely, he was easily persuaded because so much of the false claims fits his socialist ideology. He tried to walk back his commitment by jokingly suggesting he was not promoting population control. He said, "Some think, excuse me if I use the word, that in order to be good Catholics, we have to breed like rabbits . . . but no." He later apologized for his comment.

On a trip to the Philippines, where he presided over the largest mass in history, the Pope said, "It gives consolation and hope to see so many numerous families who receive children as a real gift of God. They know that every child is a benediction." He called "simplistic" the belief that large families were the cause of poverty, blaming it instead on an unjust economic system. "We can all say that the principal cause of poverty is an economic system that has removed the person from the center, and put the god of money there instead."

This comment appears to show further lack of understanding, created by an idée fixe. Ironically, both the IPCC and the Pope fail to recognize the proven dynamics of the demographic transition. The Pope continues to argue for radical new financial, economic, and environmental systems to avoid human inequality and ecological devastation.

On February 18, 2015, the Global Catholic Climate Movement officially announced the Lenten Fast for Climate Justice. Their goal, they said, "is to raise awareness on climate change" as well as for Pope Francis's Lenten call to confront "a globalization of indifference" and to spur world leaders to "work out a binding agreement to stave off rising temperature levels."

"The essential message is reduce our carbon footprint and increase our spiritual footprint," said Jacqui Rémond, director of Catholic Earthcare Australia.

Catholics from forty-eight countries and one US territory (Guam) signed onto the climate justice fast and rather than asking each country to hold a continuous forty-day fast, the climate fast operated in a pass-the-baton fashion, with a different country asking Catholics on their country's day not only to abstain from food, but also to incorporate carbon-limiting behaviors as well: walking, biking, or using public transportation in lieu of a car; working from home; using less electricity or water. The group said they were encouraging fasters around the world to share statements, testimonials, and videos explaining how climate change has affected their homelands.

Rémond further said the fast would call Catholics, as citizens of one of the highest per capita emissions countries, "to play their part" as an act of solidarity to address climate change. "It's important for Catholics to lead on climate justice, as it has on other peace and justice issues."

In his 2015 Lenten message, Francis said, "It is important to raise awareness that climate change is a moral and spiritual issue, not a political issue."

Maryland Governor Martin O'Malley said about the fast in a press release, "Uniting people of all faiths is the principle that we are called upon to be good and responsible stewards of God's creation." Patrick Carolan, executive director of the US-based Franciscan Action Network, said, "The global climate fast, in addition to the upcoming papal encyclical on the environment, has a similar effect in uniting Catholics behind the need for serious action on climate change."

In April of 2015, the Pontifical Academy of Sciences and the Pontifical Academy of Social Sciences issued an astonishing document entitled, "Climate Change and the Common Good," subtitled, "A Statement of the Problem and the Demand for Transformative Solutions." The document states,

> Unsustainable consumption coupled with a record human population and the uses of inappropriate technologies are causally linked with the destruction of the world's sustainability and resilience. Widening inequalities of wealth and income, the world-wide disruption of the physical climate system and the loss of millions of species that sustain life are the grossest manifestations of unsustainability. The continued extraction of coal, oil, and gas following the "business-as-usual mode" will soon create grave existential risks for the poorest three billion, and for generations yet unborn. Climate change resulting largely from unsustainable consumption

by about 15 percent of the world's population has become a dominant moral and ethical issue for society. There is still time to mitigate unmanageable climate changes and repair ecosystem damages, provided we reorient our attitude toward nature and, thereby, toward ourselves. Climate change is a global problem whose solution will depend on our stepping beyond national affiliations and coming together for the "common good." Religious institutions can and should take the lead in bringing about that change in attitude towards Creation. The Catholic Church, working with the leadership of other religions, can now take a decisive role by mobilizing public opinion and public funds to meet the energy needs of the poorest 3 billion people, thus allowing them to prepare for the challenges of unavoidable climate changes. Such a bold and humanitarian action by the world's religions acting in unison is certain to catalyze a public debate over how we can integrate societal choices, as prioritized under UN's sustainable development goals, into sustainable economic development pathways for the twenty-first century, with a projected population of 10 billion or more.[105]

The document then lists a litany of proposed and recommended measures for humanity to adhere to in what they call "climate mitigation." Here is that list:

- Reduce worldwide carbon dioxide emissions without delay, using all means possible to meet ambitious international targets for reducing global warming and ensuring the long-term stability of the climate system. All nations must focus on a rapid transition to renewable

---

[105] http://s3.documentcloud.org/documents/2068632/climate-change-and-the-common-good.pdf

energy sources and other strategies to reduce CO2 emissions. Nations should also avoid removal of carbon sinks by stopping deforestation, and should strengthen carbon sinks by reforestation of degraded lands. These actions must be accomplished within a few decades, reaching net-zero carbon emissions by around 2070.

- Reduce the concentrations of short-lived climate warming air pollutants (dark soot, methane, lower atmosphere ozone, and hydrofluorocarbons) by as much as 50 percent, to slow down climate change during this century, and to prevent a hundred million premature deaths between now and 2050 as well as hundreds of millions of tons of crop loss during the same period.

- Prepare especially the most vulnerable 3 billion people to adapt to the climate changes, both chronic and abrupt, that society will be unable to mitigate. In particular, we call for a global capacity building initiative to assess the natural and social impacts of climate change in mountain systems and related watersheds, and in highly vulnerable dryland regions.

- The Catholic church, working with the leadership of other religions, can take a decisive role by mobilizing public opinion and public funds to meet the energy needs of the poorest 3 billion to better prepare them to cope with impending climate changes and more generally to raise the incomes, education, healthcare, and quality of life of the world's poorest under the aegis of the Sustainable Development Goals.

- Over and above institutional reforms, policy changes, and technological innovations for affordable access to renewable energy sources, there is a fundamental need to reorient our attitude toward nature and, thereby, toward ourselves. Finding ways to develop a sustainable relationship with nature requires not only the engagement of scientists, political leaders, educators, and civil societies, but will succeed only if it is based on a moral revolution that religious institutions are in a special position to promote.

The document goes on to suggest some things we can do "beyond climate change":

- We must find ways to protect and conserve as large as possible a fraction of the tens of millions of plants, animals, fungi, and microorganisms that make up the living fabric of the world. We depend on them for the maintenance of the sustainable properties of the earth and for virtually every facet of our existence, and yet we have recognized only a very small fraction of them up to the present date. If we don't save them now, we clearly will not be able to save them later.
- In view of the continued destruction of the environment, we support and endorse the call for the adoption by 2015 of new universal goals, to be called Sustainable Development Goals (SDGs), and planetary-scale actions after 2015.
- Only through the empowerment and education of women and children throughout the world will we be able to attain a world that is both just and sustainable. We have a clear moral obligation to do this and will benefit greatly by succeeding in this goal.

Planetary scale actions? A global regime under a global authority? Sound familiar?

On April 28, 2015, UN Secretary-General Ban Ki-Moon met with Pope Francis at the Vatican and later addressed senior religious leaders, along with the presidents of Italy and Ecuador, Nobel laureates, and leading scientists on climate change and sustainable development. The next day Ban Ki-Moon responded to a question from the Catholic media, when he was asked what his views were on those members of the Catholic community who had reservations about the Pope's position on climate change. "Religion and science are united on the need for action on climate. I don't think faith leaders should be scientists—I'm not a scientist. What I want is their moral authority. Business leaders and all civil society is on board with the mission to combat climate change. Now we want faith leaders. Then we can make it happen."

On June 18, 2015, in an unprecedented move, the Pope put his moral authority behind a radical environmental agenda of the United Nations, when Vatican leaders released his environmental encyclical,[106] a letter traditionally addressed from St. Peter's Square to the more than 1.2 billion Catholics across the globe, as well as "to every person living on this planet." Though Popes since Paul VI in 1971 have addressed environmental degradation, "Laudato Si" was the first encyclical to focus primarily on creation care, the Christian idea that God gave humans the earth to cultivate, not conquer. The unprecedented 184-page papal paper, subtitled, "On Care for Our Common Home," laid out the need for a partnership between science and religion to combat human-driven climate change. The Pope said

[106] http://w2.vatican.va/content/francesco/en/encyclicals/documents/papa-francesco_20150524_enciclica-laudato-si.html

in his sharply worded manifesto, "Doomsday predictions can no longer be met with irony or disdain." In his climate action plan he chides climate skeptics for their "denial." He goes on to say, "We are witnessing a 'disturbing warming' of the earth, and humans are largely to blame for a dramatic change in the climate and nothing short of a 'bold cultural revolution' can halt humanity's spiral into self-destruction. The Earth, our home, is beginning to look more and more like an immense pile of filth." .... He states, "climate change presents a moral imperative" "... climate change is mainly caused by human action."

In the stunning papal climate action plan, the Pope begins by cataloguing a host of ills wracking the planet: dirty air, polluted water, industrial fumes, toxic waste, rising sea levels, and extreme weather. The Pope's "10 commandments on climate change" goes on to declare, "Destroying the natural world for our own benefit is a 'sin' against God and future generations." He then calls for everyone on earth to go through "ecological conversion."

The encyclical sections on climate do not arise out of Pope Francis's own knowledge but from unsourced claims passed on by his advisors.

"The sections on climate change, quoted directly from the IPCC, contained in the encyclical are riddled with vigorously debated, if not outright false claims. Here are four relevant facts Pope Francis would have known had he known the field, followed by one common-sense (and scientific) inference:

1. Computer modeling, not real-world observation, is the only basis for fears of dangerous man-made global warming.
2. On average, the 110+ computer climate models on which the UN Intergovernmental Panel on Climate

Change (IPCC) and other climate alarmists rely simulate more than twice as much warming from enhanced atmospheric CO_2 content as was actually observed over the relevant period (and even much of the observed warming is likely due to other causes).

3. If the models' errors were random, their simulations would be randomly distributed above and below observations. Instead, over 95 percent simulate more warming than observed. This indicates two things: First, we still don't actually understand how the climate system responds to enhanced CO_2. Second, the models' errors are driven at least in part by bias. Modellers believe enhanced CO_2 will warm the atmosphere by so much, so they rig the models to yield that.

4. None of the models simulated the complete absence of statistically significant global warming over the past 16 to 26 years (the RSS satellite data support 18.5 years).

5. Any climate policy can be justified only on the grounds of rational expectations about future climate response to human activity. Models can provide those rational expectations only if they are validated by real-world observation. But in this case, the models not only are not validated but are invalidated—falsified—by real-world observations. The models are wrong. Therefore they provide no rational basis for predictions about future global temperature, and no rational basis for any policy whatever."[107]

---

[107] E. Calvin Beisner, PhD, National Spokesman of the Cornwall Alliance for the Stewardship of Creation, personal correspondence to author.

"The practice of hyperbole extends throughout the Encyclical including the heading for the section on climate change labeled 'Pollution and Climate Change.' This idea introduces the incorrect link made in comments by President Obama about "carbon pollution." The Intergovernmental Panel on Climate Change (IPCC) and the Encyclical identifies CO_2 as the major cause of climate change, but CO_2 is not a pollutant. The distorted headline provides context for disturbing evidence that the Vatican does not know its science. His position is a matter of faith not facts, evidence, or science. With great irony, lack of knowledge about the sun is central again. Item 23 of the Encyclical shows the Pope and his advisors do not understand the science and, therefore, cannot understand how it is misused. Unfortunately, the Vatican seems keenly unaware that "variations in the earth's orbit and axis" known as the Milankovitch Effect, are not included in the IPCC Reports or their computer models.

"Volcanic activity" is included in the AR 5 (the IPCC's Fifth Assessment Report) under the heading of "Aerosol Burdens and Effects on Insolation." They comment, "Clouds and aerosols continue to contribute the largest uncertainty to estimates and interpretations of the earth's changing energy budget. The quantification of cloud and convective effects in models, and of aerosol-cloud interactions, continues to be a challenge."

In Chapter 9, "Evaluation of Climate Models" they report on the gap between model results and reality. The great concentration of greenhouse gases the Encyclical identifies includes carbon dioxide, methane, and nitrous oxide. The IPCC knows these represent approximately 4 percent of the total greenhouse gases and are only 2 percent of all atmospheric gases. They also know that water vapor is by far the most important greenhouse gas. They acknowledge that their list is only gases affected by human activity, and they know that restriction is by design. The IPCC was directed only to examine human causes of climate change."[108]

The encyclical implies that the Vatican has no clue about what the IPCC studied. Limitations on IPCC studies were primarily created by the definition of climate change they were given, and they result in the very restricted nature of their conclusions. They are either ignorant or they simply don't care that many of the IPCC predictions are wrong. The reality is, if the predictions are wrong, the science is wrong. As a result, the position of the Vatican as set out in the Encyclical is a matter of faith, not science. The Vatican and the IPCC are saying in unison that it doesn't really matter what the science says, we need these policies.

Spanish-born American Philosopher George Santayana famously said, "Those who do not learn from history are doomed to repeat it." The Pope's Papal Encyclical announcing the Catholic Church's decision to join the scientific claims that humans are the major cause of global warming and denounce climate scientists who oppose the claim, came almost exactly 400 years after Galileo was denounced to the Roman Inquisition in the spring of 1615. The Catholic Church only acknowledged the errors of their actions, their last and most negative brush with science, when they forgave Galileo in 1992. Pope John Paul said labeling Galileo a heretic and confining him to life imprisonment was an error. It only took 377 years for the Church to catch up with reality. No doubt Galileo is delighted, assuming he made it to heaven. It appears that they didn't learn from history. As

---

[108] Dr. Tim Ball, correspondence to the writer.

Mark 12:17 (King James Version) says, "And Jesus answering said unto them, Render to Caesar the things that are Caesar's, and to God the things that are God's. And they marvelled at him."

Shockingly, the Pope says, "Although it is true that we Christians have at times incorrectly interpreted the Scriptures, nowadays we must forcefully reject the notion that our being created in God's image and given dominion over the earth justifies absolute domination over other creatures."

Perhaps the so-called Vicar of Christ on earth might want to read Galatians 1:8, "But even if we or an angel from heaven should preach a gospel other than the one we preached to you, let them be under God's curse!" The Pope also might want to read Genesis 1:26–30:

> Then God said, "Let us make mankind in our image, in our likeness, so that they may rule over the fish in the sea and the birds in the sky, over the livestock and all the wild animals, and over all the creatures that move along the ground. So God created mankind in his own image, in the image of God he created them; male and female he created them. God blessed them and said to them, "Be fruitful and increase in number; fill the earth and subdue it. Rule over the fish in the sea and the birds in the sky and over every living creature that moves on the ground." Then God said, "I give you every seed-bearing plant on the face of the whole earth and every tree that has fruit with seed in it. They will be yours for food. And to all the beasts of the earth and all the birds in the sky and all the creatures that move along the ground—everything that has the breath of life in it—I give every green plant for food." And it was so.

The Pope has joined the United Nations in a new sustainable development agenda that must finish the job and leave no one behind. This agenda, to be launched at the Sustainable Development Summit in September 2015, is currently being discussed at the UN General Assembly, where Member States and civil society are making contributions to the agenda with broad participation from major groups and other civil society stakeholders. There have been numerous inputs to the agenda, notably a set of Sustainable Development Goals proposed by an open working group of the General Assembly.

Here are a few key sustainable development goals that are being proposed so far. The following is a template for a radically expanded "global governance" taken directly off the United Nation's own website.[109]

Goal 1: End poverty in all its forms everywhere

Goal 2: End hunger, achieve food security and improved nutrition, and promote sustainable agriculture

Goal 3: Ensure healthy lives and promote well-being for all at all ages

Goal 4: Ensure inclusive and quality education for all and promote lifelong learning

Goal 5: Achieve gender equality and empower all women and girls

Goal 6: Ensure access to water and sanitation for all

Goal 7: Ensure access to affordable, reliable, sustainable, and modern energy for all

Goal 8: Promote inclusive and sustainable economic growth, employment, and decent work for all

Goal 9: Build resilient infrastructure, promote sustainable industrialization, and foster innovation

---

[109] http://www.un.org/sustainabledevelopment/sustainable-development-goals/.

Goal 10: Reduce inequality within and among countries

Goal 11: Make cities inclusive, safe, resilient, and sustainable

Goal 12: Ensure sustainable consumption and production patterns

Goal 13: Take urgent action to combat climate change and its impacts

Goal 14: Conserve and sustainably use the oceans, seas, and marine resources

Goal 15: Sustainably manage forests, combat desertification, halt and reverse land degradation, halt biodiversity loss

Goal 16: Promote just, peaceful, and inclusive societies

Goal 17: Revitalize the global partnership for sustainable development

Pope Francis, in lockstep with the United Nations, plans to launch a brand new plan for "managing the entire globe" at the Sustainable Development Summit on September 25–27, 2015. This new sustainable agenda focuses on climate change and other topics such as economics, agriculture, education, and gender equality. For those wishing to expand the scope of "global governance," sustainable development is the perfect umbrella because just about all human activity affects the environment in some way. The phrase "for the good of the planet" can be used as an excuse to micromanage virtually every aspect of our lives as a framework for managing the entire globe.

Immediately ahead of the official opening of the UN Summit for the adoption of the post-2015 development agenda in September, Pope Francis will give an address to the United Nations General Assembly. All of this will be a lead in to the "really big show" in Paris in December 2015 where they surely intend to close the deal and adopt the post-2015 development agenda, if all goes according to their plan. Global politics and global religion are acting in one accord as per the objective—one-world government.

All this is not surprising because the main "scientific" advisor to the Pope is Dr. Schellnhuber, founder of the Potsdam Institute for Climate Impact Research. Schellnhuber, who was also appointed by Bishop Marcelo Sanchez Sorondo to the Pontifical Academies of Science, is a pantheist, that is, a person who believes that nature is a divinity and the earth is a divinity that must be worshipped at all costs. At a Copenhagen climate meeting in March of 2009, Dr. Schellnhuber told the crowd, "In a very cynical way, it's a triumph for science because at last we have stabilized something—namely the estimates for the carrying capacity of the planet, namely below 1 billion people." Schellnhuber, who has advised German Chancellor Angela Merkel on climate policy, is a visiting professor at Oxford. Schellnhuber's philosophy fits the Gaia mentality very well, eradicate 6 billion of those pesky humans. That the Pope would align himself with a pagan pantheist who believes there should be a maximum of one billion people speaks volumes.

It is easy to see what the grand green scheme is really all about. Francis is being placed in a position of global authority and the scenario is unfolding perfectly according to script; into the Kabbalist, or Jewish mysticism, one-world religious system of the Antichrist kingdom-come. That is the harsh reality and there is no way around it. It is clear to see that the Pope is pitting human beings and nature against each other. Over the last two decades, every major religious group has made environmental protection a priority in one way or another. From using solar power for houses of worship to advocating for limits on greenhouse gases, religious leaders have framed the issue as a moral imperative driven by their faith's teachings. Among the most prominent has been Ecumenical Patriarch Bartholomew I of Constantinople, spiritual leader of the world's Orthodox Christians. Francis said he read Bartholomew's writings as part of his research on the encyclical.

The Pope has gone an extra step that other pontiffs before him have not. In an unprecedented move, he has endorsed a specific UN climate treaty provision, and that is the pivotal game changer from other Vatican statements of the past. The Pope and the Vatican are confusing Catholics and the world at large into thinking that their position on global warming is now part of the moral imperative to adhere to this unholy alliance of greening the planet, including population control, sterilization, development restrictions, etc.

The Vatican and the UN are basically saying it doesn't really matter what the science says, we need these policies. After all, it's for the greater good. God Himself urges decisive action on protecting the environment, right? Wrong. Sadly, most people, even Christians, are duped into the idea that we must all "Go Green" according to Francis 3:16. This coming from the guy who declares blasphemous statements, such as everyone is redeemed through Jesus, including atheists. He said that as long as they "do good," they are going to heaven. After all, who cares if they don't believe in God, as long as they "do good." That's odd, Francis, it's not what the Bible says at all.

Statements from the Pope, the Vatican, and the referenced organizations in this book sound eerily similar to the statements from the UN report called "Shared Vision" from the 1988 Global Forum of Spiritual and Parliamentary Leaders for Human Survival, which was founded by the Temple of Understanding, and their devilish agenda to help "illuminate the beliefs of Gaians."

It is clear that the United Nations, the White House, academia, the Vatican, and others are complicit in peddling this insidious green theology under the guise of the moral imperative, but what they really want is the formation of a global authority. In the book of Hosea, God says, "My people are destroyed through lack of knowledge" and Ephesians 5:6 says, "Let no man deceive you with vain words." We would also be wise to heed the advice in 2 Corinthians 6:17, "Wherefore come out from among them, and be ye separate and touch not the unclean thing."

The only option is to come to terms with that reality and respond accordingly and "Come out of her, my people." (Rev. 18:4).

CHAPTER 12

REPLACING GOD WITH GAIA

Today the green gospel of the environmental movement is the largest and most influential social phenomenon in modern history. From relative obscurity just a few decades ago, it has spawned thousands of organizations and claims millions of committed activists. Reading the newspaper today, it is hard to imagine a time when global warming, resource depletion, environmental catastrophes, and saving the planet were barely mentioned. They now rank among the top priorities on the social, political, and economic global agenda.

Consider what was used as the invocation at the Earth Summit in Rio de Janeiro in1992: "From the point of light within the mind of God; let light stream forth into the minds of men. Let light descend on earth . . . . The purpose which the masters know and serve . . . . Let light, love, and power restore the plan on earth."

The "source of light" in the Great Invocation is Lucifer and "the Plan" intends to implement world government and religion grounded in occult powers. The creed is part of the Great Invocation based in Theosophy. Theosophy is a blend of eastern and western religions, most closely aligned with Vedic Hinduism. Although the Theosophical Society originally started in New York in the late 1800s, it was not until Alice Bailey, a hard-core Luciferian, broke away from the society in the early 1900s and created Lucifer Trust, that it gained power in America. The Lucis Trust, (formerly Lucifer Trust) is the Publishing House that prints and disseminates United Nations material. It is a devastating indictment of the New Age and Pagan nature of the UN. Lucifer Trust was established in 1922 as Lucis Trust by Alice Bailey as the publishing company to disseminate the books of Bailey and Blavatsky and the Theosophical Society. The title page of Alice Bailey's book, *Initiation, Human and Solar* was originally printed in 1922 and clearly shows the publishing house as "Lucifer Publishing." Bailey changed the name to Lucis Trust, because Lucifer Trust revealed the true nature of the New Age movement too clearly. At one time, the Lucis Trust office in New York was located at 666 United Nations Plaza and was a member of the Economic and Social Council of the United Nations under a slick program called "World Goodwill." In an Alice Bailey book called *Education for a New Age*, she suggests that in the new age "World Citizenship" should be the goal of the enlightened, with a "global world federation."[110] This is surprisingly echoed in the Pope's encyclical as he pushes for a one world global authority. Lucis Trust's sponsors, among others, are the UN and Greenpeace International. "The Plan" referred to in the above speech is taken from Alice Bailey's twenty-four occult books. The concepts of "New Age" and "The New World Order"

---

[110] Constance Cumbey, *The Hidden Dangers of the Rainbow* (Los Angeles: Vital Press, 1985), 49.

had their origins in these books. Bailey claims that Djwhal Khul, her ascended master, wrote the books through her while she was in a trance using occult automatic writing. According to occultists, Ascended Masters are supposedly superhuman beings who are part of an exalted hierarchy of demigods that secretly guide the affairs of humanity. The occult has a rank obsession with summoning the power of these ancient demigods or "god-men."

The writings of noted Satanists Manly P. Hall, a high-ranking freemason, Albert Pike, and Madame Helena Blavatsky all portray the same Luciferian theme throughout, a fascination with these gods and goddesses. As I pointed out earlier, Cathedral of St. John the Divine in New York City is another example of celebrations where the goddess Gaia is exalted. The cathedral has housed several radical new age groups at various times, one of which is the Temple of Understanding. The temple, whose interfaith purpose is the "re-integration of the sacred into our lives through universal spiritual wisdom," collaborated with the UN's Global Forum of Spirituality and Parliamentary Leaders and co-founded the National Religious Partnership in 1992. One of their leaders said, "How people of faith engage the environmental crisis will have much to do with the future of the well-being of the planet and with the future of religious life as well."

In the last decade, with the help of Al Gore, the National Religious Partnership has sent out environmental literature to over 97,000 congregations in the West and to some 100 million plus congregants, calling for the church to make the protection of earth a central message of their churches, even giving out grants for churches who "Go Green." Even the Evangelicals have jumped aboard with the Evangelical Climate Initiative

(ECI), a campaign by US church leaders and organizations to promote market-based mechanisms to mitigate global warming. ECI's first statement, calling for reductions in carbon dioxide emissions, was initially signed by eighty-six evangelical leaders. Signatories included Rick Warren, Council of Foreign Relations (CFR) member and senior pastor of Saddleback megachurch in Lake Forest, California, the presidents of thirty-nine evangelical colleges, and the leader of the Salvation Army.[111] The number of signatories had risen to over 100 by December 2007, and as of July 2011, over 220 evangelical leaders had signed the call to action. David P. Gushee, a professor of Christian ethics at Mercer University, helped draft the document.

When the Evangelical Climate Initiative launched in February 2006, the National Association of Evangelicals (NAE) was not ready to make such a commitment. Not quite a year later, the NAE worked with the Center for Health and the Global Environment at Harvard Medical School to bring scientists and evangelical Christian leaders together to mitigate climate change. As ABC News reported: "Notably, the dialog has the endorsement of the National Association of Evangelicals, which represents 45,000 churches and 30 million churchgoers in the United States."

It is tragic that evangelical Christian leaders have bought into the most devilish scheme in modern history—the green agenda. The evil Marxist cabal and their minions will not rest until they achieve total global control—politically, economically, socially, militarily, and spiritually. They won't halt until they have abrogated and nullified your own personal and religious freedoms. Rapidly melting polar icecaps, rising sea levels,

[111] http://www.nytimes.com/2006/02/08/national/08warm.html? pagewanted=all&_r=0.

increased global temperatures, and destruction of the entire species and other mantras are designed to promote fear and dread among humans to point of killing themselves. The green movement is steeped in population control tactics under the guise of "saving the planet" from the real enemy—mankind.

Environmentalism is an elaborate $100 billion a year levy that is bankrolling global government and lining the pockets of the likes of George Soros, Strong, and Gore. The issue isn't the issue. Environmentalism has nothing to do with saving the environment. People could not "save" the earth, even if they wanted. The climate has been changing since God created it and they know it. Man is trying to play God by changing this scenario. God is not waiting for us to solve the problem of global warming and climate change. We are waiting for Him to solve the problem of the global curse with His return. Reverence does not pertain to things but to persons. Efforts like the Green Gospel are revering the impersonal creation more than a personal God. God indicts those who worship the creation instead of its Creator.

Like a cancer, the green gospel is spreading through thousands of churches and organizations throughout the world, many of which have no idea what they are advancing because it is cloaked in the seemingly benevolent "going green" mantra of the day. The "church of climate change" is spiritual deception to shift the focus of the Gospel of Jesus Christ to the Gospel of Gaia.

Few Christians today are aware that the cry to "save the earth," be "sustainable," and "live in harmony with nature" is deeply entrenched in the ancient pantheistic religions that dominated the Egyptian, Babylonian, Grecian, and Roman Empires.

Gaia worship is diametrically opposed to Christianity and makes no allowance for one true God who created all things of nature. Instead, pantheistic Gaia worship is rooted in the premise that all earth and all of nature is god, comprised of many gods and goddesses, who demand total worship and obedience from every human. Failure to do so will evoke the wrath of these gods. These pantheistic beliefs have gradually dominated the environmental policies of the USA, the UN, the Vatican, and now the world. The United Nations Global Diversity Assessment not only demonizes monotheistic beliefs, but singles out Christianity as the true culprit, saying, "Societies dominated by Christianity have gone farthest in setting humans apart from nature." The UN asserts that earth must be protected from mankind, at all costs.

Just when we think there can't be another movement to invade our church pulpits, we find one waiting in the wings. So while we've had our fill of "seeker-sensitive," "purpose driven," emergent heresy, church-growth nonsense and mystical madness, we now have to brace ourselves for the "church of climate change."

The Global Green Gospel is not biblical, yet there are tens of thousands of very willing pulpits that have cooperated in recent years, with many more following suit. Gullible pastors, leaders, and congregants are willingly swallowing the "green gospel," all in the name of "saving the planet." This false doctrine seeks to pollute once-solid pulpits and to distract church members from the things that matter, such as the true gospel message of Jesus Christ and the cross. The fundamental principle behind the astonishing green global plan is rooted in the idea of "Out with God" and "In with Gaia." The plan includes all men and women bowing down to "things," to idols, in fealty to a god of their own creation.

The ultimate message of the Bible is not one of doom and gloom, but rather the hope of redemption when Christ returns. The church and the earth itself will be redeemed by Jesus Christ, the Lord of the universe. We have this blessed assurance and hope through the return of our Lord Jesus Christ to set up His Kingdom. We must protect our Christian values, which are under attack from radical environmentalists who seek to destroy the fundamental principles of Western civilization.

The destruction of America's founding principles can be directly traced to the country's willful rejection of the Bible as the source of divine authority. In the West, we have done more than expel God and the Bible from schools; we have removed God and the Bible from our very way of life. America's founding documents are themselves predicated upon God and the Bible. The Declaration of Independence states, "[Men] are endowed by their Creator with certain unalienable Rights, that among these are Life, Liberty, and the pursuit of Happiness." It also states that these rights are "self-evident" and that they constitute the "Laws of Nature." These principles are taken directly from the Bible. God, not government, grants liberty as seen in Galatians 5:1. The "pursuit of happiness" is found in the third chapter of the book of Ecclesiastes. Virtually every one of the ten articles contained in the Bill of Rights has biblical foundation. The First Amendment recognizes the natural right of freedom of speech, religion, and assembly. Christians are clearly given divine instruction regarding each of these responsibilities.

Our founding documents properly established a government designed to "secure these rights." Therefore, under the First Amendment, Christians are free to preach the Gospel of Jesus Christ and to assemble for worship. Therefore, when citizens, especially Christian citizens, allow their elected representatives to ignore or violate these founding documents, they are in essence allowing them to destroy the very basis and foundation of our country. The West is being radically transformed into a soulless, ungodly Marxist society. America is not the last bastion of freedom; it is the first and the only one. For that, it is under attack as it represents everything the Founding Fathers envisioned, a "nation of free people under God." The people I have introduced you to throughout this book envision a "one world under Gaia."

In the very first chapter, we talked about the core of Marxism and socialism being grounded in envy. Satan has always been envious of God and His creation. In fact, so much so that in the ultimate form of egotistical self-exultation Satan tried to take over God's throne. It was the ultimate coup d'état that earned Satan a one-way ticket out of heaven and into hell as his final destination. The devil is the ultimate counterfeit and manipulator. The green agenda is not about being a good environmental steward, but it is rather a very malevolent tactic used by Satan to advance his evil end time agenda on earth, sending his emissary, the Antichrist, to rule as a global dictator. Mankind has always been in Satan's crosshairs from the time Adam and Eve walked in the garden. Satan wants to take as many as he can into the burning lake of fire and he will continue to victimize humanity in every way he can devise until he is thrown into eternal damnation.

One day soon we will see the return of our glorious King, Jesus Christ. The truth is that Jesus Christ is not a way, He is the only way. Jesus Christ of Nazareth, the Son of God, is the only force that can stand against the force of evil, protect us, and guide us into God's kingdom. All other roads are dead ends. You need to be sure you are right with the Lord Jesus Christ, who paid the tab for your eternal life, nailing your sin to the cross of Calvary.

The Green Gospel is one of the greatest deceptions of our day. Environmentalism has in fact become a new religion. While the evil green movement continues to resort to manufactured environmental crises to push their pagan agenda, the Bible reassures us that the earth's climate is under God's benevolent control. The earth and man are God's creation. God created the earth for man and gave us dominion over the earth. So if the Green Shepherd turns up in your pulpit, please speak up and tell your pastor you would rather hear an emphasis on the Lord Jesus Christ, the "Good Shepherd," and His burden for lost sheep, not the "Green Shepherd" and his burden for climate change.

Will you worship the Creator or the creation?

Let no man deceive you with vain words: for because of these things cometh the wrath of God upon the children of disobedience. Be not ye therefore partakers with them. For ye were sometimes darkness, but now are ye light in the Lord: walk as children of light: (For the fruit of the Spirit is in all goodness and righteousness and truth) proving what is acceptable unto the Lord. And have no fellowship with the unfruitful works of darkness, but rather reprove them . . . . See then that ye walk circumspectly, not as fools, but as wise, redeeming the time, because the days are evil. Wherefore be ye not unwise, but understanding what the will of the Lord is.

(Eph. 5:6–11, 15–17 NIV)

EPILOGUE

"The Earth is the LORD's, and the fullness thereof."
　　　　　　　　　　　　　　　　　　—Psalm 24:1

The Bible—the sixty-six books of the Old and New Testaments—is the sole, absolute, inerrant epistemological basis for mankind for all knowledge of all things, seen and unseen, and that all claims of truth and moral duty that contradict it are false and harmful. The only true God—a spirit infinite, eternal, and immutable—revealed Himself in creation (which He made out of nothing and includes both physical and spiritual things), the Bible, and His one and only Son, Jesus Christ, and that though God reveals His wisdom and power in the creation, He is, always has been, and always will be absolutely distinct from and transcendent over creation, which He rules at all times and places. When God had created Adam, He placed him in the garden of Eden to cultivate and guard it (Genesis 2:15). It should be affirmed that godly human dominion over the earth means men and women, created in the image of God, laboring freely and lovingly together to enhance earth's safety, fruitfulness, and beauty, to the glory of God and the benefit of our neighbors. It is important to reject atheism (there is no God), pantheism (everything is God), humanism (God is to the universe as the human soul is to the human body), animism (there are many gods, and they indwell and animate physical objects as human souls indwell and animate human bodies), and any other view that denies the Creator/creature distinction, because those who hold them exchange the truth about God for a lie and worship and serve the creature rather than the Creator, who is blessed forever (Romans 1:25). Societies built on atheism, pantheism, humanism, animism (also called spiritism), or any other rejection of the Creator/created distinction cannot flourish intellectually, morally, aesthetically, and materially.

The idea that the material cosmos—"nature" and its parts, the created world of time and space, matter and energy, planets and stars, energy and material elements—is personal, either in its whole or in its parts is unbiblical and unholy. For this reason, we deny that forests and trees, mountains and rocks, oceans and lakes and streams, and animals are persons.

God made man, male and female, in His own image (Genesis 1:26–27). No other terrestrial life form bears the image of God or is of equal value or priority with human beings (Matt.10:29–31). The earth is the LORD's, He has also given it to men (Ps. 115:16) and mandated that they be fruitful, multiply, fill the earth, subdue it, and have dominion over everything that lives in it (Gen. 1:28). It should be vehemently denied that human dominion over the earth is, in principle, sinful, and that the possibility of its abuse negates the righteousness of its proper use. The earth and all its physical and biological systems are the effects of God's omniscient design, omnipotent creation, and faithful sustaining, and when God completed His creative work, it was "very good" (Gen. 1:31).

By God's design, earth and its physical and biological systems are robust, resilient, and self-correcting, and are not fragile.

We should not embrace the idea that godly human dominion entails humans being servants rather than masters of the earth. Nor should Christians accept the idea that the Garden of Eden represents that man is to "worship" the garden or the earth. The idea that, as many environmentalists put it, "Nature knows best" should be abandoned and we need to understand that the Bible normally associates wilderness or wildness with divine judgment and curse (Ex. 23:29; Lev. 26:22; Deut. 7:22; 1 Sam. 17:46; Isa. 5:2–4; 13:19–22; 34:1–17; Jer. 50:39; Lev. 16:21–22). Wilderness is the not best state of the earth. God placed minerals, plants, and animals in and on the earth for His pleasure, to reveal His glory and elicit man's praise, and to serve human needs through godly use (Gen. 2:5–16; 4:22; Num. 31:21–23; Job 38–41; Ps. 19:1–6; Ps. 104).

It is contrary to Scripture to think that recognizing instrumental value in the earth and its various physical and biological components dishonors God or is idolatrous. One way of exercising godly dominion is by transforming raw materials into resources and using them to meet human needs. The idea that leaving everything in the earth in its natural state is proper biblical stewardship (Matt. 25:14–30) directly contradicts Scripture.

Man is accountable to God's judgment in all he does with the earth. It is unbiblical to think that man's accountability to God justifies abolishing private property (Ex. 20:15, 17), adopting collectivist economic institutions, or delegating to civil governments—whether local, national, or global—ownership or control of land, natural resources, or private property.

Human multiplication and filling of the earth are intrinsically good (Gen. 1:28) and, in principle, children, lots of them, are a blessing from God to their faithful parents and the rest of the earth (Ps. 127; 128). We should reject the notion that the earth is overpopulated and that godly dominion over the earth requires population control or "family planning" to limit fertility.

When the Bible speaks of God's judgment on human societies because they have "polluted the land," the "pollution" in mind is consistently not chemical or biological but moral—the pollution of idolatry, adultery, murder, oppression of the weak, and other violations of the moral law of God expressed in the Ten Commandments (Ps. 106:38; Jer. 3:1–10; 16:18).

Environmental policies that address relatively minor risks while harming the poor—such as opposition to the use of abundant, affordable, reliable energy sources like fossil fuels in the name of fighting global warming; the suppression of the use of safe, affordable, and effective insecticides like DDT to reduce malaria in the name of protecting biodiversity; and the conversion of vast amounts of corn and other agricultural products into engine fuel in the name of ecological protection—constitutes oppression of the world's poor. Private ownership of land and other resources is the best institutional economic system for environmental protection. Collective economic systems are not good at protecting or improving natural environments. Socialism, fascism, communism, and other forms of collectivist, expansionist government offer very poor solutions to environmental risks. Limited, free, constitutional governments with market economies are good solutions.

Truth-telling is a moral obligation and sound environmental stewardship depends on it.

"The only thing necessary for the triumph of evil is for good men to do nothing."—Edmund Burke

Are you saved? What must you do to be saved?

It is time now.

If you have not already given your heart to the Lord Jesus Christ, it is time that you do so.

It can be done this very moment. I am going to ask you to read the words below and say them out loud. I am going to ask you to believe them in faith with all your heart. If you will do so, you will receive the free gift of salvation that Jesus bought for you.

Pray out loud the following:

Dear God in heaven,
I come to You today as a lost sinner. I am asking You that You save my soul and cleanse me from all sin and unrighteousness. I realize in my heart my need of salvation, which can only come through Jesus Christ. I repent for my sins now, and I accept Christ into my heart, and I receive what He did on the cross at Calvary in order to purchase my redemption. In obedience to Your Word, I confess with my mouth the Lord Jesus Christ as my Savior and I believe in my heart that God raised Him from the dead. You have said in Your Word, which cannot lie, "For whosoever shall call upon the name of the Lord shall be saved" according to Romans 10:13. I have called upon Your name exactly as You have said, and I believe that right now I am saved. Amen.

If you have sincerely prayed these words above and believe in your heart upon the Lord Jesus Christ, then at this moment you are saved and your name is now written in the Lamb's Book of Life.

Congratulations on the most important decision you have ever made.

Please know that Jesus truly does love you.

"For God so loved the world that he gave his one and only Son, that whoever believes in him shall not perish but have eternal life"
—John 3:16

Feel free to contact the author:
www.sheilazilinsky.com

Contact Information

To order additional copies of this book, please visit
www.redemption-press.com.
Also available on Amazon.com and BarnesandNoble.com
Or by calling toll free 1-844-2REDEEM.

CPSIA information can be obtained
at www.ICGtesting.com
Printed in the USA
FSOW01n1746161015
12281FS